Methods and Procedures of Outdoor Photography

To Julie Hickey

Best wishes + here's
to Good Shooting

John Warnack

Uncle John

Other Works by John Womack

The Dancing Trail
Titan Tales
Macon County Trails

Methods and Procedures of Outdoor Photography

Nature Photography in the Southern Blue Ridge Mountains

John Womack

Soliloquy Press, Franklin, North Carolina, USA

Methods and Procedures of Outdoor Photography

Nature Photography in the Southern Blue Ridge Mountains

By John Womack

Published by:
Soliloquy Press
383 Stamey Mountain Road
Franklin, NC, 28734, U.S.A.

Library of Congress Cataloging-in-Publication Data
Womack, John
Methods and procedures of outdoor photography: Nature photography in the southern Blue Ridge mountains / John Womack
p. cm.
1. Outdoor photography. 2. Nature photography.
3. Mountains North Carolina. 4 Mountains Georgia.
I. Title
ISBN 0-9655546-1-9

First Edition. 97-092291

All photographs, illustrations and cover design by the author.

Mountain Pathways &
Dancing Trail Photographic Gallery and Studio

This book is dedicated to the great
photographers who will make the great
photographs
in the Beautiful Mountains.

Table of Contents

List of Illustrations

Acknowledgments

With a very grateful and humble heart I thank the many people who helped me in the writing and publishing of this book, especially my wife, JoAnn, who did a lot more than just proofreading, going far beyond any call of duty providing encouragement and significant suggestions. Looking back on the book, I can feel her presence on every page. Marie Mellinger has been very kind to teach so many of us so many things about these beautiful mountains that she loves so much. Many of us call ourselves "Marie's girls", and "Marie's boys", too. Mike Manos and Dee Kennedy, along with other artists read portions of the book, providing recommendations and suggestions, and I am grateful for their advice. Finally, I thank my students. The art of good teaching lies in the ability to ask important questions, and my students have consistently asked the really hard ones!

John Womack
Franklin, North Carolina,
August, 1997

Chapter One

Opening the Shutter

On a bright October afternoon, high in the southern Blue Ridge Mountains, a lone hiker climbs along an open trail. He walks past mountain ash trees loaded with bright red berries, past maples with leaves that are spotted red and yellow, past great beech trees already orange and shimmering in the breeze. If you were there you might notice that he is carrying a camera and a long tripod.

Still he continues, climbing up where the oaks of a great wind forest rise high against a rocky ridgeline. There he pauses and opens an old book. After consulting several pages, he turns and walks along a narrow rocky trail that winds below a stand of Fraser Firs. Finally, he stops and sets his tripod on the far end of that ridge, high above a great blue valley now gilded with red and gold. He sights through his camera and takes readings, and writes in that old book again. Changes are made in the camera settings, and you watch as he approaches his camera as it sits on the tripod, then backs away and approaches the lenses, then backs away, and then back to the rear of the camera, and you could get the feeling that he is dancing, and in a way, he is. Then he lines up a certain view, makes some entries in his old book, and waits.

The mountains of the southern Blue Ridge comprise an area that includes northeastern Alabama, north Georgia, northwestern South Carolina, western North Carolina, eastern Tennessee and part of southwestern Virginia. They include and surround the Great Smoky Mountain National Park and several major national forests. This is *your* land and it is part of your heritage, no matter where you live or where you have come from. It is open and available for you to visit and see and to wander upon, and it is one of the greatest treasures of this planet. While the term "Smoky Mountains" is often used synonymously with the Southern Blue Ridge, in fact the Smokies combine with the Balsam, Nantahala, Tusquitee, Unicoi, Cowee, and Snowbird Mountains, together with others, to constitute the southern Blue Ridge Mountains. Some call it the Great Blue Wall. The Cherokees sometimes called this area the Great Blue Mountains of God. Anyway you look at it, you carry your camera here into a land that is filled with wonder, beauty and awe. These are the oldest mountains of the world. Marie Mellinger, the naturalist who worked with the early Foxfire series, has pointed out that its forests are the "mother forests" of the planet. From the seeds of these great forests came the foundations for most of the trees of the world. It has been said that there are as many varieties of trees in the Southern Blue Ridge as are found in all of Europe; and more than 1,300 plants are native to these mountains. It is a land of astonishing beauty and variety, but it is not at all easy to photograph!

This manual is intended to help people make good photographs in these mountains, and it is primarily directed to three general groups of photographers:

First, are those who shoot with relatively small cameras such as basic 35mm equipment, APS, point-and-shoots, disposable cameras and similar equipment. While these cameras may not be able to apply the instructions about exposure adjustment, f/stop modification and so on, the suggestions concerning composition, color, landscapes, wildflowers, lighting, tone and texture can enhance the images produced by any camera. The second group includes photographers who work with more sophisticated equipment, usually 35mm, that often have automatic exposure and focus capability, interchangeable lenses and many technologically advanced features. Sometimes these photographers are puzzled that their expensive equipment seems baffled when working in these hazy mountains, and can yield photo after photo that is lifeless, washed out and featureless. This manual can show how to interpret the information their equipment is providing them, and also how they might consider certain artistic techniques that can help elevate their photography to a new level.

Finally, there are the more experienced photographers who often use larger and more elaborate equipment such as view cameras, medium or larger format equipment etc., who are already proficient in photography, but who are not familiar with the special photographic problems presented by these mountains. Hopefully, they can find hints and suggestions here that can help them apply their extensive skills and experience to this challenging photographic arena.

I started teaching outdoor photography classes in Franklin, North Carolina, when the community college at which I taught economics and business courses decided to offer a continuing education class in outdoor photography. I volunteered to teach the course, but it did not "make" because only nine students registered. Some of the students were upset. Two of them claimed they had waited for eight years for such a class. So we all agreed to proceed without the benefit of the college. That was my first photography class. One of the first problems we encountered was that there was no text book. My students asked me what I did besides photography and teaching. I told them I was a writer. They said: "Write a textbook!" So I did. I "published" that first one through a local printshop, keeping roughly one class ahead of the students, and this is the offspring of that book, although now extensively rewritten. It is really the third edition, but it is the first one to *actually* get published. There is another photography book lurking in my computer which may follow this manual in a couple of years, and which would be a bona fide textbook, complete with questions, answers, practices and problems. This manual should also serve the purpose of classroom instruction, although it is intended to be carried in the field or used as a reference by individual photographers.

Meanwhile, I have continued to teach the course that I call "Methods and Procedures of Outdoor Photography" on my own, first from a local church, then my home, from the mountains themselves, and now from my own *"Dancing Trail"* art studio and gallery in downtown Franklin.

Many of my students have been artists in watercolor or oil mediums. Some of them are familiar with cameras and photography and wonder what went wrong, why their pictures have turned bad since they moved here. As I said earlier, the mountains are not easy on photographers and good photographs are sometimes hard to come by. Yet some of the most beautiful pictures made on this planet have been made right here! How did that happen?

Are there certain tricks that you can use? Well, probably, but tricks are unreliable and tend to work both ways. Good photographers get their great pictures by applying and refining the basic fundamentals of photography and by composing their pictures as any artist would compose a work of art. They seek to reflect what they "feel" by selectively arranging the things they see into a harmonious whole. We will pursue that process in this manual as we explore what we need to know about the camera, study how to make composition work for us and not against us, learn how to use principles of color to make our photos leap into brilliant life, and consider how we can adapt our photography to the constantly changing lighting conditions so we can still get great photos whether the day shines brilliantly under bright clear skies or lies mysteriously hidden under a dark and heavy overcast.

The wild places - oceans, deserts, mountains and forests - are necessary to our planet so that it may clean and replenish itself. People need to know that such places exist, that they are in danger, and that those special places have an intrinsic value far greater than what they are worth just in dollars! It seems that the beginning of this new century will be a crucial time for those wild places that so stir the human spirit. Powerful governmental and commercial interests, local, national and international, now seem dedicated to the destruction of these places so that they may be liquidated and converted into short-run profits. One can almost sense a gigantic "Going Out of Business!" sale: "Last Days for this Sale", "All Items Must Go!" "Hurry - Hurry - Hurry!" Yes, there is a dark side: that we might need photographs of these wonderful places so posterity will know what we traded for dollars. But most importantly, I really believe that we cannot destroy that which we know and love.

I have been asked why I seem to want competitors for my own business. I reply that my "business" is the production of images that carry the feelings and moods of wild places. I know I am not alone in this mission, but I also know that we need help! And I look forward to a day when great hoards of outdoor photographers, and other artists and writers swarm upon the mountains, deserts, prairies, and beaches everywhere and create art that will help lift the human soul and the consciousness of all people higher than our highest mountains!

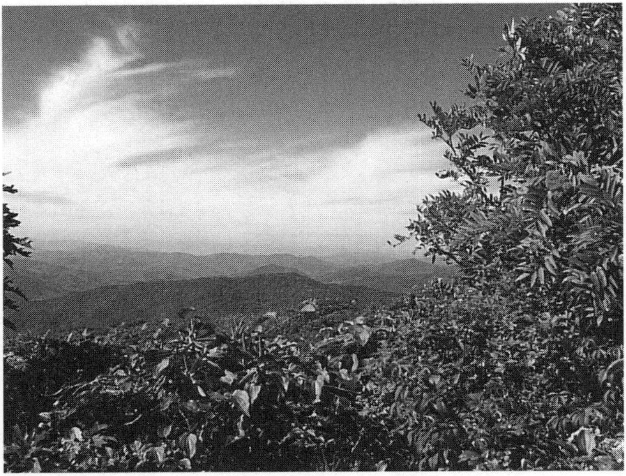

FIGURE 1.1 VIEW FROM STANDING INDIAN MOUNTAIN, Macon County, North Carolina.

Chapter Two

Design & Technical Composition

Is composition really important? I've talked to artists (watercolor and oil, as well as photographers) who say they never concern themselves with it. Are they just kidding? Do they use it unconsciously perhaps, or accidentally? And then there are people who *do* use it "religiously" and their work looks like they are painting by numbers. So what is this thing we call composition? And *is* it really important?

The answer is that composition is the heart and soul of all art. Its purpose is to make the viewer a participant in an act of creation. It is a communion. And more than that: is an invitation to the dance!

Good composition will attract the eye of the viewer to the picture. It will call forth the viewers' imagination, lead it into the photo, show it around, and keep it there. It will do the work of a guide, and set a pace and cadence for viewing the picture. Good composition will unify the different objects and elements, provide a resolution and harmony to the photo, and set a rhythm to which the viewer can respond and contribute their own feelings. Good composition will create a desire on the part of the viewer to share the feelings that the picture conveys and to participate in those impressions. Art is not just a presentation; there must also be an internal interpretation and a response. You know good composition when you hear your favorite music played right, and sung right - you just can't help but join in and sing along - and you may hum the tune the rest of the day! That's good composition, and you can do the same thing with your photographs!

The artist looks at the universe. That part of the universe that is visible at any given time might be called the artist's "View". This View, no matter how beautiful it may seem to be, will usually not make a good photograph because it is filled with an infinite variety of constantly changing elements and possibilities. Any View, however, may be composed of several "Scenes". A Scene is a portion of a View that contains, or may contain, a harmonious collection of Objects, Subjects and other elements that can evoke an "Impression". An Impression is a nonphysical quality, feeling, emotion or mood. That Impression might be called the *mystery* Subject which is sought by all true artists, and it will determine how the visual elements will be designed into a framework capable of supporting a work of art. That framework which supports the art is called "composition".

In general, composition is concerned with the selection and arrangement of all the artistic elements present in a Scene into a design, and the determination of the relationship that the elements and the design will bear to the Subject. Normally, there will be only one visible Subject in a good photo; all other elements and Objects seen in the photo will be secondary to that Subject, and they should all emphasize, modify or support it. If they do, they are **part of the composition**, if they don't, they are distractions, or clutter. Remember though, a really creative work of art has two Subjects. One will be the physical Subject that is visible in the photographic Scene; the other is the Subject we sometimes call the *mystery* Subject, and that is the Impression evoked by the Scene or View. These two Subjects must support each other.

Good composition is never just a simple set of rules. Various competent artists will render the same Scene into different pictures that reveal images not otherwise noticed, and which will create feelings within the viewer, and even other artists, that they possibly overlooked when viewing the original Scene. Composition takes place on at least *four* different levels: 1) **Design** Composition, 2) **Technical** Composition, 3) **Interpretive** Composition, and 4) **Expressive** Composition. All four of these compositional concepts can be grouped together under the general aegis of "Composition".

1) Design Composition consists of arranging the Subject and secondary elements in certain gener-

ally acknowledged design formations so they form shapes, lines and curves, patterns, color mixtures, balance, location and similar relationships with each other and the Subject. 2) Technical Composition will interplay with the entire range of photographic skills and equipment capability including viewpoint, framing, metering, perspective, lighting, tone, color, texture, focus, film choice, accessory equipment, etc. 3) Interpretive Composition consists of seeking, understanding and responding to the impressions that speak to the artist through the scene, in the form of space, moods, time, dimensions, environmental context, ambiance, emotions, feelings, sentiment, intuition, impressions and so on. 4) Expressive Composition embraces the presentation of the art and relies on skills of storytelling, juxtapositions of planes, synthesis of impressions, use of archetypes and myths, suggestion, reflection, symbols, associations, revelation, illusion, etc.

This chapter will discuss concepts relative to the first two levels of Design and Technical considerations. Chapter three will discuss Interpretation and Expression.

CONVENTIONAL COMPOSITION DESIGNS:

The basic designs of Conventional Composition are not a recent product of modern photographers. They are concepts that come from the ancient past of mankind - long before Giotto, da Vinci, Michelangelo, long before the paintings in the pyramids of Egypt. The timeless art of design composition is found in ancient cave paintings that were drawn more than 20,000 years ago, long before man had invented other language. Composition has been present since man has been man. If you have not used these designs in your photography in the past, you will notice a sudden and dramatic improvement in your work as soon as you begin! People *will* notice!

However, a word of warning is appropriate. These basic designs are not in themselves art, nor is their use even the most important part of composition. The reason a great photograph or other work or art is great is NOT just *because* certain designs were used. Many great photographs and paintings, in fact, seem to ignore them, and many not-so-great pictures have sacrificed a real message to present a compositional design! A listing of these designs can represent "art" in much the same manner in which an autopsy can describe some characteristics of a once living body. "Well, let's see, here is a liver, some lungs, a heart ..." So, liver, lungs and heart *are* very important, but just putting a liver, lungs, heart, etc. into a bag will not create a living being! On the other hand, most living beings do *have* liver, lungs and heart, and most great art *does* employ some of these designs. Now, having said that, let's look at some of those basic designs, at least one of which - sometimes more - are commonly found in good art:

1) Unsymmetrical Division. It is very easy to put the Subject of the photo directly in the center of the frame. However, such a composition often renders a flat and confusing photograph. If the Subject is in the center of the photo, the viewer's eye will tend to wander, looking for a guide, or hint, or some kind of a message. The concept of Unsymmetrical Division suggests the placement of

the Subject or an element of the picture to one side of the center and higher or lower than the center of the frame. Not only does such a placement help attract the viewer's eye, but it helps to lead it in the direction the photographer wishes it to go. Often it is possible to place a vertical element such as a tree on one side of the frame, and a horizontal element such as a pathway or horizon near the top or bottom of the frame. This is a more complex form of Unsymmetrical Division, and is very effective since it seems to place an inner "frame" within the outer frame and gives visual references that can more easily attract and lead the eye and imagination into your photograph. (See figure 2.1) Also, when a horizon is included in your photograph, it will probably be more effective if placed in either the upper one-third or lower one-third of the frame rather than in the center.

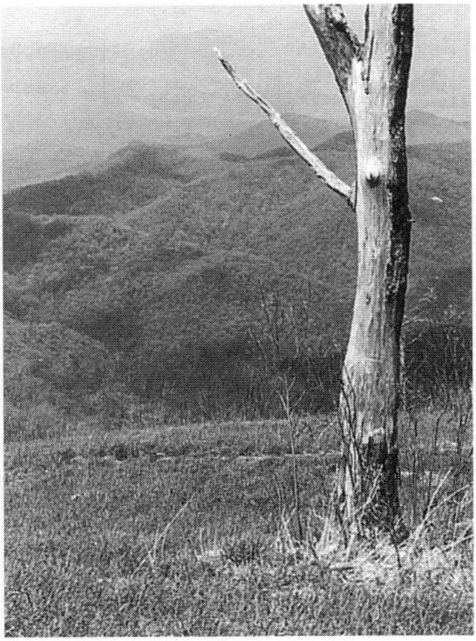

Figure 2.1 Unsymmetrical Division. View from Siler Bald.

2 Rule of Thirds. This rule is based on a belief that when a line is broken into two unequal

parts, the shorter part should bear the same proportion to the longer part as the longer part bears to the combined length of the two parts. Divide the photographic frame (in your imagination) both horizontally and vertically into thirds. This will provide a "grid" with four intersections. (See figure 2.2) These four intersections are referred to as "areas of inter-

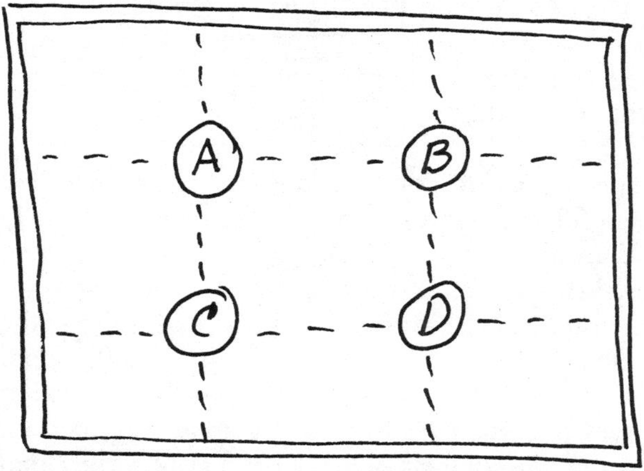

Figure 2.2. Rule of Thirds
The intersections

est" and are often identified by the upper case letters "A", "B", "C" and "D". The letters are placed in the manner in which we read a page, with "A" being in the upper left, "B" in the upper right, "C" in the lower left, and so on. The subject, or main point, might be placed in one of the four intersections, and one or more of the remaining three intersections would have some kind of a supporting element. It is not necessary to place something in *all* four axis. One is usually enough, often you can get two axis covered, and sometimes three. Usually, by the time you get all four covered, one or two of the elements will be a shadow or a minor object. The rule of thirds also states that the upper left "intersection" (the one we labeled "A") is the most powerful for westerners since those people normally read from left to right and top to bottom. I often teach, and sometimes use in my own photographs, this "rule" a little differently. I mentally divide the frame into four equal quadrants: upper left, upper right, lower left and lower right. (See figure 2.3) For ease of reference, I refer to these areas as Quadrant A, (upper left), Quad B, (upper right), QC (for Quad C, lower left), and QD (lower right), again, the order in which we normally read a page. Then I will place a Subject or Objects in the center (or near the center) of one of these quadrants. This will introduce an error of about 10% away from the center, compared with the "Rule of Thirds". For this reason I will then move the elements closer to the center to achieve the harmony that can come from use of the Rule of Thirds. The more precise we are in design composition, the better chance we give our photographs to present the impression we want to express. Normally I try not to place the Subject of the photo in QA. Since the viewer's eye will tend to search

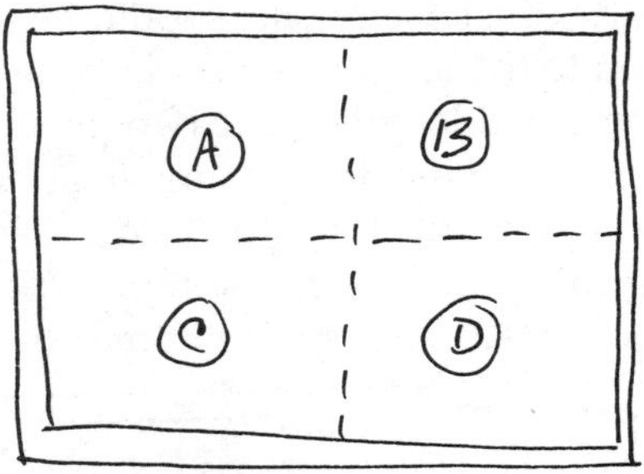

Figure 2.3. Rule of Thirds
The Quadrants

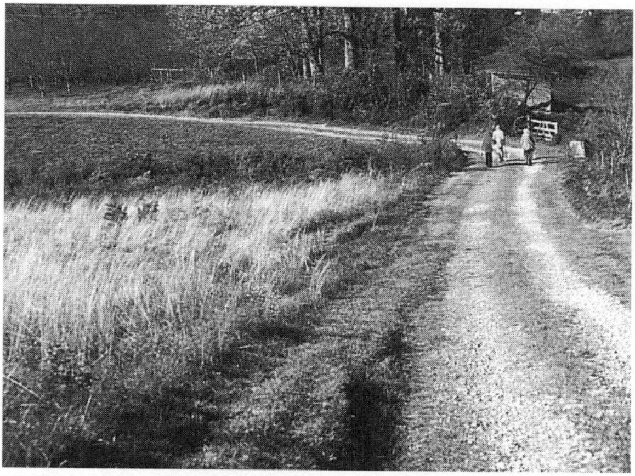

Figure 2.4 Rule of Thirds
Notice how the eye is guided from QA to QB, where the subject is. Then from QC to QB, and later from QD back to QB again.

there first, I would prefer to place an Object there which will serve as a pointer to guide the viewer, and help them "remain in the photo" and engage them on a search . (See Figure 2.4).

3) Shapes or forms. Natural shapes and forms can be integrated beautifully and dramatically into your pictures. Shapes are two-dimensional figures such as **triangles, circles, squares, rectangles, and other odd and interesting shapes,** and they help to attract the eye and especially the imagination of the viewer and to guide them through the elements of the photo. Note that not all of the shape needs to be within the frame of the photo, just enough to establish the presence of the shape. (Figure. 2.5) Often shapes are used as silhouettes. Forms are figures which appear to be three dimensional. Often

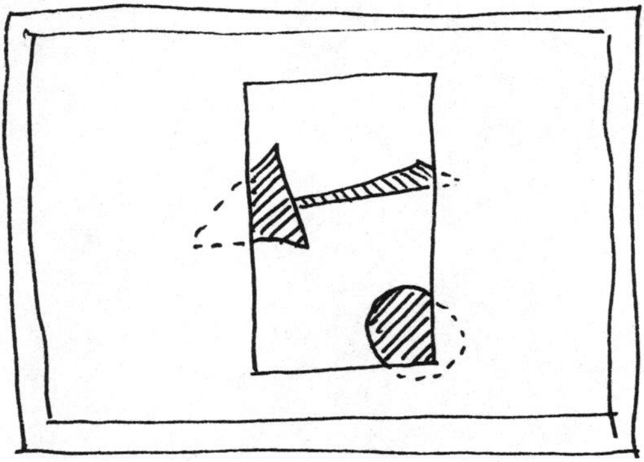

Figure 2.5 Forms & Shapes

this is effected by the use of shade and light, or by the display of texture. The art form called "still life" presents many good examples of the difference between shape and form. Forms add dimension to the photo and can serve to lead the viewer's eye in detail photography such as tree trunks, large rocks, etc. Bold forms and shapes can be thrown into collision with each other resulting in very dramatic impressions.

4) Lines and curves are very effective in directing the eye and imagination of the viewer. (See figure 2.6) Lines serve to direct attention to the subject, and can provide one or more of the imaginary lines used in the Rule of Thirds. Lines can also intersect and form angles. Curves can take the place of complete or partial circles or can just "wander". Perhaps the most effective curve is the so called **Line**

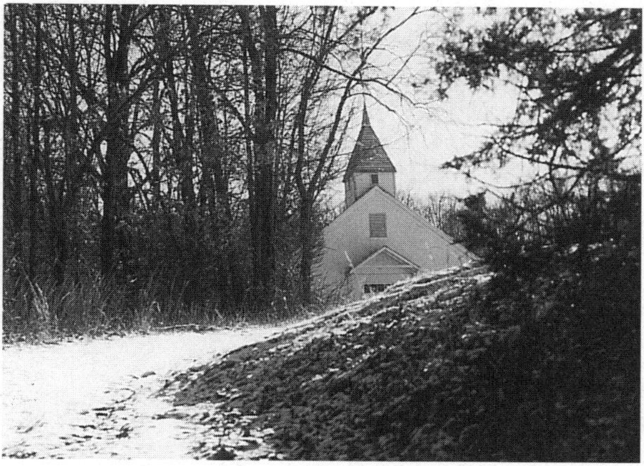

Figure 2.6 Lines and curves.

of Beauty or **Hogarth Line**, which is really just an **"S" curve**.

5) Patterns. Patterns can be **repetitious, developing**, or even just **suggested** iterations. Think of "Visual Echoes". In the beautiful mountains one can often see repeating patterns formed by the other mountain peaks when one is standing on top of one of them. Winter forests often provide a repeating pattern in the bare tree trunks. Often, it is possible to get a vertical pattern from the bare tree trunks and a corresponding horizontal pattern from their shadows. (See figure 2.7) Patterns are very effective is helping to establish moods such as power by reinforcement of a design or peace from a positive reassurance. We will study these concepts more in the next chapter. Developing or suggested patterns are those which are not completely shown in the frame, but one in which you can see patterns trying to

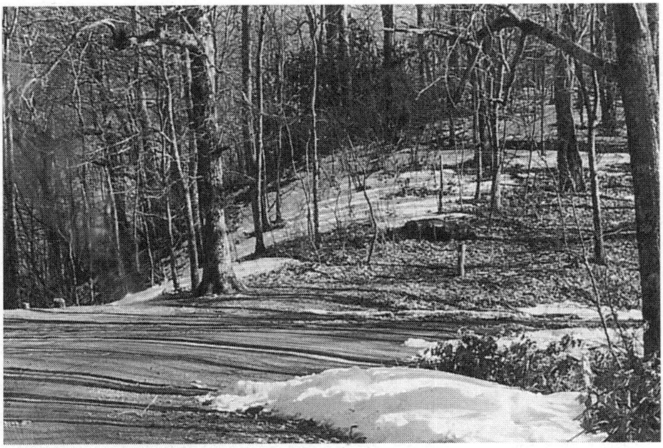

Figure 2.7. Repeating Patterns

emerge, or to develop.

6) Centralization. Sometimes, it is desirable to abandon the Unsymmetrical Division and Rule of Thirds, and put the subject or horizon in the direct center of the photo. Many photographers do this occasionally, and it is sometimes a powerful tactic in a very **"busy"** photo. The most important thing to remember when this is used is that the sides and top and bottom of the picture must be **balanced**. This is often used when mountains are sharply reflected in a clear, calm lake, or when a heavily traveled thoroughfare is shown in a crowded city. Photos like these can be part of almost any vacation. They can help portray mood, and context, and can be useful in leading up to the presentation of detail photos. Note that this reflection technique is useful **only** if the water in the lake is very **calm** and reflects the scene clearly; otherwise, use the rule of thirds or

unsymmetrical division. (If there is a slight chop on the water, try very long exposures to see if that will "hide" the chop [it will] and bring out the reflection [maybe].)

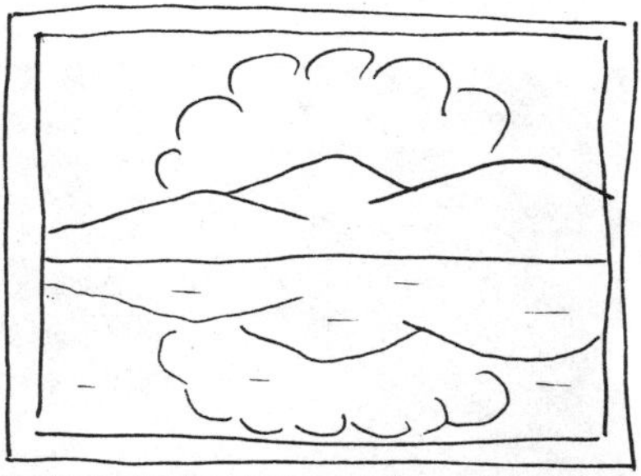

Figure 2.8. Centralization

7) Light and Dark Areas. They can work together, or confrontatively. They can provide accent to the subject or can be part of the details that are incorporated as areas of interest for the Rule of Thirds, or as shapes. They are both especially helpful to "balance" the photo, or to highlight the subject. Light areas tend to attract the "eye" of the viewer, darker areas seem to lead the viewing. Most people tend to think of "Dark" as being "heavier" than "Light", so a photo that is half "dark" and half "light" might not seem to be as effectively balanced as one that is, say, 1/3 "dark" and 2/3 "light". Also dark is perceived to "descend", while light "rises". Try some photos using lightness and darkness and see what you think. There is also a **fulcrum effect**, since "dark" near the middle or bottom of the frame adds stability, while if it is over at the edge, it will tend to induce a "tilt". Darkness is especially effective when incorporated as a **silhouette,** such as placing black tree shapes against a lighted mountainside

or sky (see figure 2.9) , and as background to lighted flowers or trees. It is a very effective "underlay" for

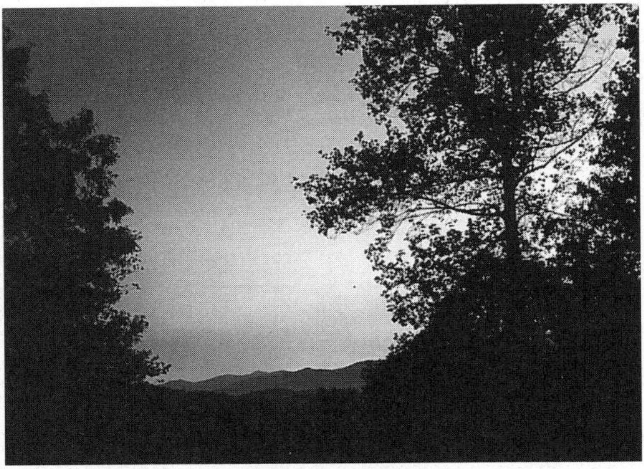

Figure 2.9 Light and Dark.
View from Stamey Mountain Road

lighted trees at the edge of a forest. It is often very effective to have an object that is light in front of a darker background or vice versa. Often, a silhouette of a branch, draped casually across the top of a frame, with its end twigs or leaves drooping slightly, can be effectively used as a guide to keep the viewer's imagination inside the frame. Used for this reason, it does not need to be sharply in focus.

(8) Movement. It is easier to direct the viewer's eye through the use of apparent movement by having the subject or object moving into the frame rather than out of it. Persons will probably look better if they appear to be looking into the frame than towards the outside. Trees or flowers that are lean-

ing, will probably look better if they appear to be leaning into the center of the photo.

(9) Axis of Direction. Sometimes a great curve may be part of your photo. That would provide an opportunity to consider construction of a "center" to that curve, and perhaps a "line of radius" stretching from the curve.

So, these are some basic rules of Conventional Compositional design. Remember that compositional elements are assembled from the secondary portions of the photo, not the Subject, and they help to emphasize, point to, or modify the Subject. We said at the beginning that we would not sacrifice art for the sake of composition, but I ask my students to do just that while they are taking this course. Once you master the techniques, and see how they look in nature, before the shot, during the composition, and in the final photograph, you will find yourself incorporating them into your work very easily. Practice making photos which use only one concept at a time so you can get experience in selecting and using different forms of composition and see their effect. But when you do serious shooting, consider using several of them in the same photograph. Don't try to use them all in every picture you take, but a combination of two or three will enhance almost any photo so that it will attract the attention and imagination of the viewer. Also vary your usage of these techniques. If every picture you make uses Unsymmetrical Division and that only, your portfolio will assume a bothersome quality about it. You may indeed wind up with a rose garden, but all the roses will seem to be the same size, shape and color.

Use of these techniques will enhance your photography immediately. But remember, our business is to make photos of what we feel, not just to make photos showing good design composition. The design composition is one part of a great dance, and if the music blows away the dancers or the dancers blow away the music, then there may be an exhibition, but there will be no art.

So, we have talked about "Subject" and "Supporting Elements"; there is a third group, probably the most common of all in photographic art. Those are the "Distracting Elements". They are anything that does not add to the photo. They can be called *Photographic Weeds*. They will ruin a good photo quicker and more completely than a poor subject arrangement, poor exposure or bad composition. Their presence or absence is often the single item that distinguishes an amateur snapshot from a classic picture. Everything in the classic photo belongs there. What is in the classic photo that doesn't belong there? Nothing! How do you get rid of the distracting elements? The first thing is the most important, and that is being able to see them while you are composing the work. The second is to practice making pictures with zero distractions or as few as possible. Look at the great photographers, they may have some distractions but they are kept to a minimum or placed in a weak place in the photo. Where do you look to see great photographs? Begin with the National Geographic magazine.

Finally, make sure that there are no "contra-composition" forces at work; like a tree growing out of the back of your subject - or a telephone pole incredibly balanced on top of the head of someone - or the kid who was graduating from middle school and was standing in front of a sign that read "Class of 85", but the photographer inadvertently cut off the first two letters of the sign. (Ruined a good photo!) And as your finger reaches for the button, plumb your frame and make sure your horizon is level or your vertical is really vertical. Little errors last forever.

TECHNICAL COMPOSITION:

It is an old and well known statement that artists are both the master and slave of their medium. If you are a watercolorist, then your technical composition will be concerned with paper, colors, brushes, sponges, knives, palette mixtures, and many other items and techniques. In photography, we have the tools of a different medium: film, light, use of focus, application of tonality, framing for the finished print, viewpoints, lenses, filters, tripods, flash equipment, and so on. Each of these items can affect the final picture and each plays an important part in technical composition. The tools will be discussed here, and will be reviewed in greater detail in chapters four, through nine.

1) Film. One of the first steps is to balance the immediate problem of quickness of image capture with the later problem of enlargement. Some film is produced with larger crystals in its emulsion, and it records images quickly. It is called "fast" film. Other film is designed to record images very slowly. Fast film tends to have a detectable "grain" in it, especially when it is enlarged beyond an 8 X 12 inch

print. "Slow film" images can be brilliantly clear. Grain is not necessarily bad. It may be very dramatic when you want to suggest mystery, but it could be a real detriment if you want to present the picture in brilliant, blazing clarity. Then, if there is not much light, there may not be much choice! Should the film be black and white, or color? If color, should it be print or transparency? If you want color, shall it be true to life, or subdued, or brilliant?

2) Focus. Just what do we want the viewer to see, and how clearly? Normally we want the Subject to be in focus, other elements can be in focus too, or totally out of focus or partially out of focus. That's up to us. Do we want the viewer not to see a certain thing at all, or do we want the viewer to have to work on a certain partly focused element and help create it in their own mind? Perhaps we can throw telephone poles and houses completely out of focus. If there are trees in the background, perhaps a significant shift of focus could blur them and suggest the presence of a large forest, by letting them be enough out of focus that they do not dominate the photograph but not enough that they are totally unrecognizable.

3) Tone. This is the element of softness and harshness, the realm of darkness and light. We can take the hand of the viewer and lovingly lead them into a gentle place of peace and joy, or we can thrust a stark scene screamingly into their face. Often, we will take great care to place a highlighted part of the photo, a flower, or leaf perhaps, against a darker area to outline it better. We will orchestrate tonal ranges much like music, so we can control the mood of the photo, bringing in at least three distinct tones of

light, preferably five, and perhaps as many as eleven.

4) Framing. This is how we choose what will be in the photograph and what we will leave behind. Almost any View has several Scenes, and we really don't want to make pictures of the Views because they don't photograph well. The Scenes are what tell the tale! Here we are no less than Noah, himself, standing at the Ark; because no matter what is present in the scene, if it doesn't get into the frame, it will not be found in the picture. Our frame is really a three dimensional "cage" of sorts in which we place and arrange the objects we want to display in the photograph. Zoom lenses really accentuate the power of this part of composition since we can expand or narrow the field of view from side to side and top to bottom with almost casual ease. We can also change the depth of focus, by changing the size of the aperture opening, and almost like playing a trombone, make the zone of focus very shallow or very deep. Our three dimensional "cage" is the frame in which we "catch" our photo.

5) Viewpoint. This is determined by the Subject and the modifying elements. Let's say there is a man, a tree and a mountain we are to photograph. Shall the man be bigger than the tree? The tree bigger than the mountain? It all depends on your viewpoint.

6) Lenses. Lenses let us magnify, distort, crop, edit. As we said in the paragraph on framing, we can greatly narrow the actual Scene, magnify it or, using wide-angle lenses, place it in a different context. With zoom lenses, we can crop and do some editing before we make the picture, and compare dif-

ferent Scenes while we stand there and before we make any photos.

7) Filters. Skylight and UV filters are used primarily to protect the expensive outer lenses of the camera. Polarizing filters can darken the sky into a deep blue color and also cut glare from grass, water and flowers. Graduated neutral density filters are filters that are dark gray on one edge, and clear on the other. They require a special mount, but once you have it in place you can move the filter up and down over the lens of the camera, placing the darkest part over a bright sky, and letting the main subject area be photographed through the clear part, and it will tame the wild sky that wants to control your landscape photos. There are some "warming" and "cooling" filters that can add a small amount of rose or blue to your pictures. Colored filters seldom work well with color film, and I do not use them with color slide or color print film.

8) Color. More to come on this in chapter four. It's technical use begins with the film selection. There are allegations that one brand of film brings out more blues and greens and another brings out more orange and yellows. Personally, I feel that has a lot to do with the color of the box the film comes in. All the big photo magazines run comprehensive tests every year, check them out at your library. Then try some out for yourself - see what you think. Other factors to consider: 1) Are you seeking vibrant color or more lifelike color. 2) If you want the color photo to last a long time, you can get a written guarantee against fading for up to 200 years from some printers.

9) Tripod. To use one or not? It will help

steady the photograph. It definitely will give much clearer shots time after time. The great problem concerning clarity of an image is not that it might be blurred, but that it might not be razor sharp. This problem of sharpness intensifies dramatically as the images are enlarged. Many *great* transparencies can make your skin crawl when they are enlarged to 8 X 12, or 16 X 24. The tripod <u>always</u> helps. It also permits a sharper use of focus than might be otherwise possible, since you can go to lower aperture sizes, extending the time of exposure. It can also let you use a slower speed film for still greater clarity in the final photo. Perhaps the best use for the tripod is in the framing of the shot. It is about the only way you can really get the edges of the picture just right. It is really difficult to make a great outdoor photo without a tripod. (See the chapter that discusses photographic equipment.)

10) <u>Flash</u>. It brings its own palette of problems and opportunities. I will sometimes carry one when hiking on a dark day in dark woods, on a windy day, or if I am using very low speed film in the forest. You can always get a photo, but it may not be the one you were hoping to get. Then again, it may be really dramatic.

11) <u>Bracketing</u>. Bracketing is a technique of exposing a picture at the optimum settings indicated by your exposure meter, then shooting another exposure with the settings changed to admit more light into the camera, and a third shot with the settings changed to admit less light than the optimum setting. Such a procedure would be called a "three-shot bracket". How much more or less light should be let in? Usually changing either the shutter speed

or aperture opening to its next setting will do the job. Sometimes you might want to bracket as many as five shots by shooting the first one "on"the indicated exposure settings, the second shot at the next slower speed, the third shot retaining that slower shutter speed but with the aperture opened up one setting, then the fourth shot at one shutter speed faster than that recommended by your exposure meter readings and the aperture on the recommended setting, and the fifth shot with the faster shutter speed retained and the aperture closed one stop down below recommended. It's actually done a lot easier than it sounds, and if there is a problem with shutter speeds due to Subject movement, you might want to move your aperture settings through two different settings up and down, or vice-versa if you are bumping up against an aperture setting limit and shutter speed is not a problem. Bracketing is often done with slide film and to a very much less degree with color print film. See chapter eight for more information about this procedure.

11) Other equipment. There is a lot left that we are not going to talk about in this manual. Bellows, extension tubes, teleconverters, and etc., etc. But they all can help you advance your mastery (and servitude) of the art.

Chapter Three

Composition: Interpretation & Expression

In the last chapter we talked about basic techniques of picture design and some of the technical aspects of photographic composition. Those basic elements of composition would be applicable to any art form. The design forms would be the same in all picture preparations, and the technical procedures would vary depending on whether the artist were a sculptor, watercolorist, photographer or writer. Both are basically independent of the subject matter or the story to be told, and relate more to the "science" of being an artist. In this chapter, we will discuss how we can interrelate with the scene we are photographing and with our future viewers. This involves an emotional attachment or involvement between nature and people. If we can call chapter two the "science" of art, we might call this chapter the "romance" of art!

INTERPRETIVE COMPOSITION:

Great pictures tell stories of things that really can't be seen. These are the "*mystery subjects*" we mentioned back in chapter two. They often refer to the great ideas such as Beauty, Love, Friendship, Power, Duty, and Joy. Often they will portray deep emotions like Despair, Loss, Gain, Sadness, Happiness, Ecstasy. Nobody gets these *mystery subjects* on film any better than sport photojournalists. Forget the home runs and touchdowns, get that look of rapture on the face of the guy who did it; or the stunned dejection on the other side!

In outdoor photography, the pace is usually different. A View appears that seems to speak to you, or there is a Scene that is compelling. What do you do next? You might begin by asking yourself what "messages" are you receiving from the Scene? What feelings are calling to you? What is there that is coming through beyond that physical aspect that you visually see? One thing you know is that you sense a non-physical quality, a feeling, emotion or mood that was perhaps evoked by an object, Scene or a View.

Often, pictures that are composed quickly do not carry their messages well; good composition takes time. Great composition is the product of careful preparation. Here are some steps we can do to help get ready:

1) Preparation First, we can clear our mind of other thoughts. This enables us to concentrate on the physical View we observe and seek the Impressions we receive from that View. Then we

bring those two attributes (physical and emotional impressions) together in our mind. Now we can examine our own nature for a reaction to those impressions, and bring feelings from within us to join with the sights and emotional impressions already collected. Observe the resulting "flow" of feelings and moods and emotions between the visual Scene, the Impression received, and the reaction from yourself. Does there seem to be a sense of harmony? Or do you sense turbulence? If there is a feeling of turbulence, you might search for another Impression from the Scene or from yourself. See if this "sense" changes as you concentrate on various parts of the View or different Scenes. If you sense an impression of Peace, say, but with a small amount of turbulence, then perhaps there is a slightly different impression involved such as Joy, perhaps, or Elation. There may be a feeling of Power, or even some negative feeling that strikes a response. Must the theme of the interpretation and telling be one of the Great Ideas? No. Sometimes that is good; sometimes I just want to play. And sometimes, the best photos I make are those I made when I was playing.

You may have doubts that this will work. I encourage you to give it a try. Almost all artists *do* take part in such a communion, although often unconsciously and haphazardly. We all do it with old familiar places, such as when we return to the town where we grew up, or when we first visit places of great renown, like the Grand Canyon, or St. Peter's. Those of us who are parents do this with our children. Is it not a form of communion? Yes, it is, but often this communion is done absent-mindedly. So, why not try it intentionally?

2) Site selection. You stand out on the edge of a great universe, gazing into the soul of beauty, and if you are a real artist, you are in love. If you were more practical you might simply remark that you have found a View, a portion of the visible universe. A place of many Scenes; that is to say there are Subjects, Objects and other Elements. A practical person would probably observe that there are certain Sites at or near this View, places from which Scenes could be surveyed, and photographic equipment set up and photographs taken. A truly practical person would also notice certain Locations, or general places that could provide access to these Views and Scenes and Sites, perhaps a parking place from which Sites could be reached. A completely practical person would also probably mark such places in a log or record or a book of some kind, so he or she could get back there again, practically anytime. But would an artist do such a thing? Well... .

3) Mood or Feeling. Can you get more than just one feeling from a certain view? Sure. Very good sites often have many such possibilities. Think of Grandview Point at the Grand Canyon, for example. Try Waterrock Knob on the Blue Ridge Parkway. Or how about almost any waterfall? What is it that attracts you to the waterfall? There is that mystery subject, again. Is it grace, and balance? Perhaps. Could it be symmetry? Maybe it is the power that you can feel there. Maybe it is the freshness of the air, or the breathless race of brand-new water falling headlong through a timeless forest. If you sense power, you might consider trying to use a faster shutter speed, (at least 1/500 second, or faster) so drops of water stand out, and you might empha-

size the tilt of some downward sloping rocks. You might shoot with a greater degree of contrast to bring out more white and black in the photo, - a "good against evil" kind of thing. Another photographer, or you another time, might seek to show grace and beauty from that same waterfall. Then, you might want to use a shutter speed slower than 1/60 second to cause the water to flow together, and then bring in swirling water in a pool below the falls, or flowers, or mist floating across the pool, or new leaves, or autumn leaves. Perhaps it would be interesting to pan some shots of the water falling. Put your shutter speed on a lower speed, perhaps less than 1/30 second. Then practice picking out a drop of water and tracing it as it falls. Follow another one through the viewfinder, then, after you have the cadence, try a couple of shots. What will you get? Who knows? Perhaps you will understand the waterfall better.

4) Time. Time is a mysterious realm of memories or nostalgia. Normally, art is concerned with space rather than time. But art is an illusion that we create and share through our imagination. Time is also such an illusion. We photographers routinely compress three dimensions into two; why not capture fleeting time and pin it, all flashing and blinking, to the present moment; or take *any* moment and spin it out into immortality? The change of seasons and weather can be effective when shown together with some routine, normal, even commonplace item or event. Combinations of seasons are effective. Frost gleaming on a pumpkin, a dusting of snow on the last bell pepper of the year, or sunset on a rusty tomato hanging in a gaunt garden with twisted corn

stalks partly blurred in the background; these may carry an awareness of a summer now gone. Can there be a more incredibly joyful photo than that of daffodils climbing out through a layer of snow?

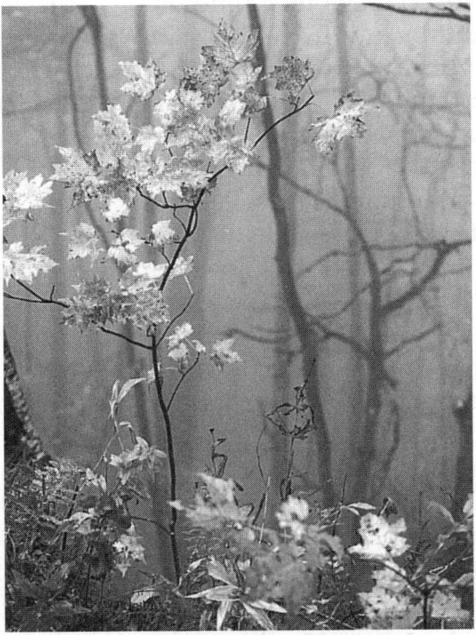

Figure 3.1 Autumn & Winter at Rock Gap, N.C.

Figure 3.1 shows a small sugar maple with a few leaves that are a brilliant shade of gold. (Hard to see in black & white!) but the twisted shapes of the bare trees behind the maple clearly tell a tale of winter creeping through the cold mountain clouds.

5) Dimensions. Going beyond the three dimensions of physical space often just means find-

ing a balance between the various elements in your picture and then removing an important reference point or landmark, inviting the viewer to participate in the work. Remember how Japanese art often brings in "space" (or what Westerners might call "nothing"), and uses that "nothing" to balance out a powerful subject? This helps to let the artist emerge from his own limitations, and later lead the viewer from his. Much of the art of Zen poetry and painting turns on what is suggested, rather than on what is clearly seen. Western artists have traditionally divided spirit from nature. Nature has been seen as wild, untamed, perhaps evil; spirit comes from heaven to subdue it. But in the Eastern world, and that of

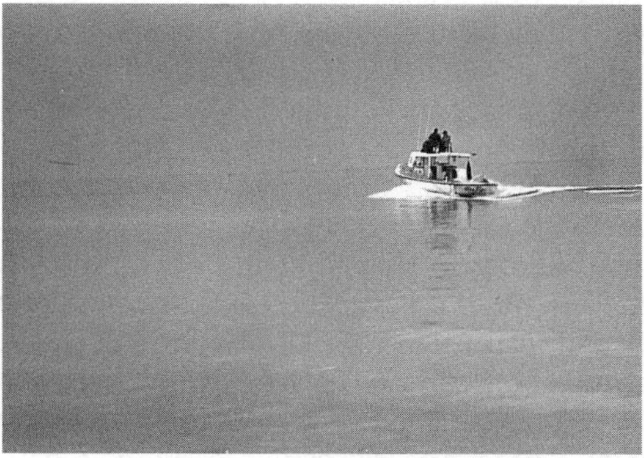

Figure 3.2 Space as a dimension.

our American Indian ancestors, spirit and nature are often a single harmonious entity. Figure 3.2 shows a boat on some errand on a lake, but it could be sailing on an ocean or through a vast sea of spirit. By the way, the next time you see an Audubon print, take a good look at the background. Notice how they are not only appropriate to the bird that is depicted, but also how they are not as graphic as the bird, and how they seem to "suggest" rather than show. Perhaps we might want to use foreshortening to photographically compress physically separated elements.

6) Mood Expansion. Just being aware of different mood elements can be powerful. We may feel loneliness, sense echoes of the past, emptiness, mystery, grief, or find places where elements can echo or resonate. Show this to the viewer, and emphasize the feelings. Suggest what lies beyond. Invite the viewer to participate by filling in the missing parts of the images. If your Scene has a flaw in it, partly conceal it; viewers who are interested will supply the missing element with a perfect one from their own imagination; lingerie designers know all about this!

7) Colors. Colors can alter and enhance moods with great power. More will be said about the use of color in chapter four, but we know how greens and blues are considered to be colors of rest, peace and relaxation. Green is also growth and newness while blue can also be sad. Yellow is supposedly the color of creativity. Red is reputed to be the color of conflict and curiosity. Purple is regal, the color of power and authority; black is intimidating and frightening; yet fascinating, the color of mystery. Orange is the color of play; brown, that of work. Certain combinations clash violently such as yellow and purple, orange and blue - sounds like your football team? No coincidence, you may be sure! Other color combinations immediately take us to the

Caribbean, Hawaii, Japan, or to the land of the Red, White and Blue. There is the yellow rose of Texas, blue shadows lie across the trail, and black is the color, according to an old folk song corollary, of my love's true hair. Color is powerful, and it is easy to overlook at this point in composition! What about *Colorcast*? This is the overall color tone of the View or Scene. But notice what we are talking about when we speak of Colorcast is not the individual colors themselves, but the basic palette from which they could have come. Colorcast might be called the color of the air or sky that you are shooting through. More about this in chapter five.

8) Plane Juxtapositions: Bringing together different moods or feelings. A waterfall, for example, could be photographed with a wide angle lens, that would include a close-up shot of a butterfly or dragonfly. The waterfall could be photographed in great power and the butterfly could be shown to be gentle, all gossamer and fragile. We've all seen pictures of a flower photographed on a precipice, perhaps in the Grand Canyon. What are *those* planes? The gentleness, fragility, and ephemera of the flower are placed against the great power, solidity and timelessness of the canyon. Add a little color, unsymmetrical division, perhaps the right kind of film, and you've got the makings of a great photo - that is, if the light is right!

9) "Balance" and "flow" can help you to feel a picture when you look at it. I have seen many very good photos that did not directly use any of the compositional methods discussed in this chapter, but which still have a "flow" to them, or a very special harmony. This type of composition is especially

important when photographing animals or birds, or for that matter, any detail object that will occupy a very large percentage of the frame of the final photograph. Some wildlife photographers have said that 75% to 85% of the frame should be occupied by a bird, if a bird is the Subject. In such a case, the overall "flow" of the very few supporting elements becomes critical. Let's say the bird is singing into the heavens; it would be great if he is standing on an upward sloping twig, and a few tree tops, out of focus in the background, are also lifting upward.

10) Intuition. Left-brain, right-brain; "Deep Blue", the 256-computer consortium has more logic than its chess-playing opponent, Kasparov. But without intuition, its' game is not human, and without intuition, our photographs are not human. Intuition is sometimes a still, small voice within us, but as we learn to work with it, that voice can get louder. Often, intuition, in my case, comes almost as a wish, when I look at a View or Scene. Like, "I wish I could bring out a certain element!" It's presence is often more like a fascination, perhaps, that brings us back again and again. Or maybe it is that element, itself, the one we wish were there, that *is* there and saying to us: "Here I am - Hey! Look over here!"

11) Artistic assistance: Use the work of other artists to help you prepare. Music is especially powerful for this. I prefer baroque classical music, and that fits well into my preparation and interpretation. Vivaldi's *Four Seasons* are perfect for almost anytime. In the autumn I might add Respighi's *Ancient Airs and Dances;* and in springtime, Copeland's *Appalachian Spring*. In the winter, I sometimes remember a folk song *"In the Bleak*

Midwinter", and lots of great Christmas anthems, and let all that guide some of my preparations. For summer, how about Mendelssohn's *Mid-summer Night Dream*? So, this is not a complete lineup but just a beginning. And I often carry tapes pertinent to the mission with me on a shoot and listen to them while driving from site to site. I look toward Beethoven, Mozart, Haydn, Handel, Bach, Vivaldi, Telemann and often have them available for my tape deck while driving from Site to Site.

Are you a Country Music fan? Well, there's a lot of mood and a lot of truth in that music, too. Jazz? Why not? I don't know much about jazz , but maybe photos made under its influence are long overdue. I look forward to seeing some! Will it help our shooting? I don't know, but I do know that if you listen to Vivaldi's *Gloria* during an autumn sunset from Waterrock Knob, you'll never be the same person again, even if you do come back down. (And, of course, this is all in <u>preparation</u>, I would <u>never</u> play music during such an event, even if I were the only person present. No artist, including Mozart or Haydn, can ever capture what is *really* out there, and I want to get *that* firsthand, and I give it my full attention.)

Don't forget painters; when you survey a scene, think about Cezanne, Chagall, Monet, Van Gough. You're not going to copy their technique, (if you do, your camera is in need of <u>serious</u> repair!) but how about their interpretation? You don't really know what they looked at but you can see some of their passion. Something came to them and passed through them to be liberated into expression. What's really out there? What is tugging at *your* sleeve?

EXPRESSIVE COMPOSITION:

Now let's look at how we might tell the story. Normally, we know there should be an introduction, a body and a closing. But this is a dance, remember? So what can we do as outdoor photographers to express these feelings we have just talked about?

1) Storytelling. Tell a story. Really! Write one down, preferably in outline form. Tell what you would like to have in the way of photos from your trip to the Mojave Desert. Make a scenario. What would be some great shots that you might like to get? How about your next trip to Mt. Mitchell? Get some books, brochures, maps; look at almanacs, check out trail guides. Go not as an innocent child into a strange world, but go as a student might approach a great teacher with questions and interest and real concern. This preparation, by the way, can be half the fun of the entire trip. (May even be the best half!) When you are stymied at Cowee Mountain Overlook on the Blue Ridge Parkway, write out a story of what you see, or want to photograph. What is it that you feel? It might be helpful to draw a sketch of what you feel is out there, not just what you see. Then, just like editing a rough draft, begin improving on what you have just done. Sketch on a notepad what you wish *was* there in the Scene, and when it starts to look good in your sketch,

look for its physical counterpart. It is probably hiding there!

2) Be bold. Can photographs tell a real story? Can they match up with the other artistic mediums? Yes! Photography is the most powerful and dynamic form of art known to mankind.

We have all known that the earth is part of the solar system for some time; we had seen artists' renditions of that imagined sight for more than fifty years, but when we saw that first photograph of our earth floating in space, the earth changed, and we changed. The earth could never be the same earth again.

Artists, poets and writers introduced us to the pleasures and joys of war for countless generations, and we loved it. Then Mathew Brady brought us some bad news, and war has gone down hill ever since.

We all know about how many children die of starvation every day, and we feel sorry for them. But when we see Kevin Carter's incredible photo of the starving Sudanese child, covered with flies, collapsing to the ground, still crawling in the dirt, completely abandoned except for his last earthly companion: a huge vulture, the size of the child, walking behind him, watching, waiting. We have been told that one picture could take ten thousand words to explain; here's one that would take ten million years to explain. And you don't even have to look, all it takes is a quick glance, and you can't ever be the same again as you were before you saw that. Yes, photography can be *too* powerful.

The Wizard, Ansel Adams, took us to another planet - the most beautiful place in the universe!

"Where are we?" we asked him. He pushed his glasses up on his forehead, smiled, wiped his hands on his apron, and said: "Welcome home."

You will encounter other artists out on the trail. When you set up your tripod, be kind, be quiet, and be sensitive. The painter, you may see out there is dabbing, looking for realism; the writer is searching for ten thousand words. You hold realism and ten thousand words in your hands, and you are not going to stop there.

3) Movement. Something coming or going. Clouds coming (or going). People pointing, or trees or shrubs "pointing". It could be kinetic like a waterfall or portentous, some kind of a premonition. In these mountains, up high, the season of spring can come as great power, almost as a movement, as it sends colors up the mountainside. In the autumn those colors fall with visible movement. Or it could be a great sweep of lines that move the eye with ease and authority. (Fig. 2.4 provides a sense of movement that is more based on a form of inevitability, and you can't help but sense the movement of the three figures.)

4) Surprises. What is there that seems strange and unusual in that locality. Does it say something about what else is there? If you've prepared well, you will understand what is unusual in this site. Again, think of Bach or Mozart, their music is full of surprises. How did they do that? Often it was because they combined certain things that were usually not seen as being together. Surprises come from unexpected combinations. You know a lot, you have a lot of tools, use them in ways that respond to your curiosity. One method being used

as we approach the turn of the century is an expanded use of time exposures. Try photographing flowers swaying in the breeze at 1/4 second. Use grainy film where it normally would not be considered. Use long time exposures after sundown and catch the sky making faces.

5) Conventional Designs. Use those conventional designs we discussed earlier. The proper use, or intentional disregard of, these methods can be an important method of expression in themselves.

6) Symbols. Use of symbols. What symbology seems to come through to you in the scene you are viewing? What symbols could you use to express your feelings? Joseph Campbell said that symbols are bridges between our minds and our feelings. Marshall McLuhan spoke once of making the American flag a piece of white cloth with black letters on it reading "American Flag". Then he contrasted that with the *symbol* of "Old Glory", waving in the free air. Can we do something like this? Often it a matter of testing.

7) Cartoons. Cartoons are often good at storytelling in a single picture. Usually cartoons are distinguished by their exaggeration of a certain point, and their low degree of clarity. A great icicle, for example, hanging over a winter snowcap, clearly sets the stage for that season, and also can lend a sinister aspect to the view. The art of the cartoonist is the art of abstractions that help create illusions.

8) The critical moment. There is no substitute for a good climax! Remember the photo of Clay standing over Liston? Those pictures come from one who understands what is going on and who anticipates what can happen, and especially, one who

wishes a certain thing would occur! Does the photographer actually *will* these things into existence? Probably not, but some people seem to be a lot more open to them than others. The great sports photographer gets those great shots because he knows the game. He knows what is going to happen, or what probably will happen, or maybe what he wishes *would* happen, and when it *does* happen he or she gets a great picture!

9) Point of view. Another look at the interpretive aspect of viewpoint. How about a photo of a hiker on the trail. Maybe a good profile, up close, with the mountains lying out beneath her gaze. Perhaps a view from behind the hiker on the trail. Maybe a distant view of a hiker standing on a promontory or ledge, or big rock. Or at a waterfall, a distant shot with her standing near the falls, or a closer one with the falls about the size of her body, in the background; or maybe a close up of her face, with the falls, the size of her face, in the background. It's all point of view.

10) Essay. Normally a photographic essay is a collection or collage of prints. But look at a Walker Evans photo, look at his 1935 print called *Cabin in Alabama.* Notice how he uses unsymmetrical division, from left to right, and from top to bottom - thus dividing his photo into four parts - AND there is often a story in each part! Look and see the weathered boards on the side of the house, the oil cloth on the rough table inside, the spotless floor, and the kitchen hutch in the background. Everywhere you look you see a symphony of texture, tone, dimension, time, feeling, shapes, light and dark, patterns, and things you didn't know before.

You are welcomed in and guided and made to feel at home, even though it is not his home! But it is definitely his photo. You get the feeling looking at each of his pictures that this might be the last exposure on his last roll of film, the last picture he will ever make. This is the one he wants to be remembered by.

11) The 'incidental' photo. This is a good method for candid photos of people photographed in the outdoors. Make pictures of children showing off their pets or dolls, parents showing off their children. In such a role people tend to lose their ego momentarily. Many people will do the same thing when they are showing off some prized new possession such as camping gear, a camera, or a good camping spot.

12) Blurring or freezing. When photographing moving flowers under gusty conditions at a high shutter speed, it is worth while to time the shot so that the flower is photographed when it is being blown in one direction, instead of when it is whipping back.

13) "Panning". We have already mentioned panning a drop of water at a water fall, but this can be done with falling snow, also, and perhaps even better, in the autumn with falling leaves.

14) Plane Intersections. This process was explained by Arthur Koestler, but its great master was Alfred Hitchcock. How can we forget the killer chasing the beautiful young woman to kill her, as she flees into a fair. The deadly chase goes on, she crying and running, he grimly following, and everyone else is smiling and laughing, clowns are all around, the carousels are running, and calliope music fills the air. Can we do something like this?

One question that constantly is asked, and about which qualified professional photographers constantly disagree is: shall the photo be objective or subjective? Objectivity insists that the photo contain only those elements visually present at the time of observation, and that they be faithfully rendered as they actually were physically present at the instant of exposure. This concept lies strongly within the realm of photojournalism: perhaps it is an evolutionary corollary to a trust in science (maybe the camera *does* lie; but it shouldn't!). Subjectivity, on the other hand, lies within the realm of art. It says: "Yes, I see that wart, but I also see beyond to a reality (or beauty) that is perhaps not apparent to the crowd. Here, let me share that beauty with you!"

As photographers, we sometimes do encounter circumstances which call for faithful archival rendering, and when they occur, we should weigh those responsibilities. As an artist, our commitment and our promise is to help feelings and moods emerge from the captivity of their physical form and enter into the landscapes of the human soul.

Chapter Four

Lighting, Tone & Contrast

All photographs use light as a source of their images. We know that natural lighting varies significantly from season to season, throughout each day, and sometimes even the hour-by-hour variations can be dramatic. In the southern Blue Ridge Mountains, it is common to see lighting changes of a significant degree while setting up a shot, and again as you begin bracketing. This is another good reason for always using a tripod Even if you don't need one when you begin your shot you may need it before you finish!

Without going into a study of Optics, Wave/Particle Theory, or Celestial Mechanics, what do we outdoor photographers really need to know about light? Well, most of that work has been already done for us by the people who built our cameras and made our film. All we really need to provide is our input regarding the quality of the light, the direction of the light, and how to adjust the exposure meter readings to achieve the exposure we want.

Many fine **exposure meters** are available, and they provide excellent readings of both reflected and incidental light. But, exposure meters really don't seem to fit into the mountain forests very well. Personally, I carry two cameras and two or three lenses, plus film, a filter or two, and usually a tripod. There is a limit, and like most photographers, I always seem to leave behind more than I would like to, yet also carry more than I would like to. So an exposure meter is just another expensive item that I occasionally wish I had with me. Most cameras have an excellent exposure meter already built into them, and they provide information to us that has already been converted into f/stops and shutter speeds appropriate to the film we have loaded into the camera. Unfortunately, their reading must sometimes be adjusted before we use them to make an exposure. More about that in a moment.

First, we need to analyze the quality of the light we will be using so we can see how it will affect our photos. The **quality** of the light depends on its **intensity, direction** and **color**. We will talk about color in the next chapter, now let's discuss some considerations of **intensity and direction**. First, we'll see how the **intensity** of light affects our photography.

Intensity of Light. When photographers analyze the intensity of light, they often will classify it as being *Bright, Filtered, or Dim*. These levels of intensity refer to the amount and type of light that will actually enter the camera as the picture is recorded. They are not just three arbitrary categories chosen for convenience, but are more like three basic oceans of light, each with its own opportunities and problems. They are easy to identify by their characteristics, and will determine the kind of photographs that can be made in their presence. Also, lighting conditions often vary throughout each day, and you may encounter a combination, or *all* of these conditions on any given day.

Bright light is light that comes directly from the sun, essentially unfiltered by clouds, atmosphere, trees, or structures. It is not hindered by water vapor, dust or hydrocarbons in the atmosphere. The source of bright light is readily apparent. It appears to come from a very small emission point, and its direction is clearly evident. (While we understand that the Sun is actually very large, it still only occupies 1/2 of one degree in the Earth's sky, and that qualifies it as a "point of light".) Shadows will have sharp edges and there will be stark contrast between the lighted area and the shadows. Shapes, forms and details may be lost in glare and shadow. Good photographs *can* be made under this type of light, but tonal range may be reduced into just two values: "too bright" and "too dark", and the contrast may be strong enough to cause difficulties in the photograph. This is the type of light in which the altitude of the sun is very important, and when the sun gets much above 45° to 50° above the horizon, the contrast difference between light and dark areas becomes too great for slide film. Even though some of the newer color print films have a remarkable range (often called "latitude"), all film has an ultimate limit in its ability to record both very bright and very dark objects in the same exposure and still retain detail in both light and dark areas. Often, the result will be that your exposure meter will opt for a non-existent or uninteresting "middle" and the dark areas will be too dark and the light areas will be too bright, and you can't even tell what it was you were trying to photograph! See figure 4.1 for an example of this type of problem. Texture may be difficult to even see, much less to photograph in such light because of the great tonal difference between light and dark. My polarizing filters often get a lot of use under such lighting. (See the chapter on photographic equipment.) Colors may be affected by glare if in direct light, and actually be *too* bright, and without sufficient shading or tinting, the colors may look a bit like a black and white photo which has been colorized. If an object is in the shade, its color may also be tinged with blue light (from sky) or green (from forest). If the sky is included in a photo in such a light, it may appear pleasing, and can be very blue, especially if a polarizing filter has been used. This is probably the most difficult light of all for making good photographs, but when the sun is lower in the sky, or if large contrast gaps can be avoided or spanned with some middle-range contrast, acceptable photographs can still be made. Bright light offers good opportunities for early- and late-in-the-day work. Good detail work can be done in open shade, filtered shade (such as you often encounter in the forest) is usually not good because of the contrast range. Landscapes are difficult unless there are cloud shadows laying across the mountains. See the photograph on the cover of this book, for an example. Even then the shadows may be too deep, again making the contrast range too great for good resolution. I often put my camera away during midday (10:00 a.m. to 3:00 p.m.) on such a day. That is a good time for a lunch, nap, or hiking.

Filtered light is light that has been significantly filtered by atmosphere, clouds, trees or structures. Perhaps the sky is "clear" but there may be significant aberration of the light due to water vapor, dust or hydrocarbon particles in the sky. The source of the light seems to come from a large area rather than just a spot, but it still clearly comes from a definite *direction*. This light will definitely produce shadows but they will have soft edges, and there will usually be some reflected or refracted light present in those shadows. The contrast between the light and dark areas will be clearly evident and may or may not be great enough to cause exposure problems. Usually, tonal ranges will be good under this type of light although you will have to remember to include some middle tones in your photos, or the pictures may be too contrasty. This may be the best light of all to bring out texture, although there will still have to be some compositional effort. Color and form are readily apparent although some details may be lost in dark shade, and glare may be a problem. Polarizing filters will occasionally be helpful under such lighting. The sky may or may not be pleasing if included in a photo made on a day like this. If there is blue sky or white cumulus clouds available, then they will probably photograph very well. Photography under this light may be a little difficult from time to time, buy you will probably get your best landscape pictures in this light.

Dim light is light that has been heavily diffused. The diffusion could be caused by heavy clouds, tree cover or structures, and can be encountered even on a bright sunny day if your subject is in open shade. The light does not appear to come from any direction, its source is essentially the entire sky, and it produces either no shadows at all, or very indistinct shadows. Contrast between light and dark is reduced substantially; there may be "shade", but no real shadows. Tonal ranges may be excellent, and not only will there be a middle tone available, there may be five or six tones, or levels of brightness in that middle range. Form is usually apparent, and details will usually "hold" in both dark and light areas. Colors can be very bright, and will often completely saturate the photo although some details may be muted in darker areas. Texture can be brought out well under such circumstances, especially if different colors are involved. Reflectors may be useful. If the sky is included in a photo made under such lighting conditions, the best that can be said is that it will appear milky, whitish or dirty gray; that is to say, it will not be a pretty picture. It may be worse than that, because it will be surprisingly bright and will probably flood the photo with this bright milky gray colorless light, introducing heavy contrast, and ruining the photo. Normally, I will not let the sky intrude into photos on a day like this. That often means no landscape pictures under such conditions. Graduated neutral density filters can combat sky intrusion. Remember though, that if the diffusion is caused by structures (such as in the shade of a building), and if the sky is blue, the objects that are photographed in that light will have a very bluish colorcast to them. During overcast conditions, it is possible to make some of your best detail shots (flower, trees, trunks, waterways, etc.). Some landscape pictures are possible, but the sky must be left out of them. A graduated neutral density filter can be a great help here. Photos of man-made structures, such as old barns, ruins, etc. can be very effective, again remembering the sky is a problem. On such a day the sky *can* turn "angry", and with swirling clouds, and much variance between dark and light, there is always the possibility of getting very dramatic skyscape and landscape pictures on a stormy, overcast day. Also, the overcast can vary remarkably in brightness, from being dark enough to use headlights if you are driving, to being bright enough that you may want to wear sunglasses. Sometimes, the sun will break out of a heavy overcast right at sunset, making an incredible lighting condition. Such photos really have to be anticipated, because their existence may be measured in one or two minutes - or less. Don't forget to look for and treat glare, especially when doing detail or flower work. Flower petals may photograph well, but leaves on the same plant may have undesirable glare. Polarizing filters may help this, although it will lengthen the exposure time.

Finally, can you have a day that has *none* of those three lighting conditions? Yes. The best approach under such conditions is to be aware that the basic information is still valid. That is to say, if you are setting up to shoot a flower on an overcast day and the sun comes out through a hole in the clouds, and the sunlight is shining on the flower, then you have choices to make. You can wait, or proceed with the shoot after changing settings on the camera. Or you can shade the flower with your hat, or another photographer. You may also have a better shot with some drama in it due to the unusual lighting situation, and your overall colorcast of the shot may be dramatically altered. But you will have, under mixed lighting conditions, "mixed" opportunities. You will still have to consider light source, brightness, direction, shade, contrast, tonal range, color, texture, and sky condition.

In the mountains, it is common to arrive at a good Site in heavy morning fog. Then, the sky may turn into a very dark, low overcast, and later change into a high, very bright overcast. Then, the clouds may clear, almost magically, into a brilliantly clear sky. In the afternoon, high cirrus may form, gradually becoming a high broken alto stratus with strongly diffused light. Thunderstorms can always form and bounce light all over the place, almost like the echoes of their thunder. So you may not see many "days" that fit one of the three lighting conditions, but you will see those three conditions constantly. Especially in the mountains, you must be conscious of the changing intensity of light with every shot you make because it often changes even as your shutter opens and closes.

Direction. Now let's consider the effects caused by the **direction** of light. Natural light normally comes from one of *four basic directions*: from 1) *behind the photographer*; from 2) *behind the Subject*;

from 3) either *side;* and from 4) *above the Subject.* Light coming from 1) behind the photographer tends to cancel out all shadows, provides very little contrast or texture, possibly will show shape, can be used effectively with a dark background behind the object (assuming the light doesn't reach the background). Light coming from 2) behind the Subject can render marvelous silhouette or outline of the subject, and if it is from a little above it too, then it may outline the silhouette with a fine line or aura of light. If the Subject or Objects are translucent, like autumn leaves on a tree, or a flower in bloom, or a flag, they may light up almost like neon lights, and be very effective, especially if they can be placed in front of a darker background. Light coming from 3) one of the sides will emphasize shadows, dimensions and texture. Shapes may be misleading, and Forms can be exaggerated. Some details may be obscured while others can leap right out at you. Light from 4) above, tends to flatten out the Subject and cause a loss of dimension and color tones and render the photo into its too- bright and too-dark, very contrasty components.

There is a fifth direction, and it is one that I call 45-45-R. That stands for 45° from the front of the Subject as it stands facing the camera, 45° above the Subject's horizon, and with some Reflection from the other side. Studio photographers who do portraits will often use this type of lighting for their Subjects. We outdoor photographers don't make many studio portraits, but a quick look inside one of those studios will show how portrait photographers seek "perfect" lighting conditions, often by combining three sources of light. The first would be the main lighting source (usually called the "**key**" light) and it would face the Subject at about a 45° angle from the Subject's face, and would also be about 45° above the level of the Subject's head. The second light (usually called the "**fill**" light source) would be a smaller light (often just a reflector) located on the opposite side of the Subject from the key light, and the third would be a small light behind (usually called "**background**" lighting) and a little above the Subject to provide it with a tiny "halo", or to illuminate the background. Often studio photographers will try to get the side that is lighted by the key to be about 3 times as bright as the side lighted by the fill. This is called a 3:1 **lighting ratio**. We can approximate this ratio in outdoor photography, but we may have to guess somewhat, and fine adjustment is not usually available.

So, how does all this affect us? Some of us remember the old box cameras that required all those who were being photographed to stand perfectly still, not breathe, and squint into the sun. So, most of us have a whole generation of really tense, grim-looking, two-dimensional relatives. But now we can get away from all that rigidity. We might want our photographs to have the sun about 35° to 55° above horizontal level and about 35° to 55° in front of the object. The more directly the rays strike the Subject, the clearer will be the shapes and color hues, and the more obliquely the rays fall upon the Subject, the greater the form, contrast, texture, and color tones will be revealed. Photographs of any detail Object such as flowers or boulders or trees or fellow hikers can be enhanced if the light from the sun strikes them from about 45° above, and about

45° to one side, and then there is *something* on the other side that will reflect light on to the side opposite from the sun. That *something* could be a cliff side, a large boulder, or a waterfall, or even tree cover if it will reflect a noticeable amount of light. (I cheat, and usually carry a small reflector - more on that later in this chapter.) The color of the *reflected light* would also be of interest as it could vary from gray to brown or white or green.

Any landscape will be effectively rendered if light from the sun is coming from one side and reflected light from clouds (like a thunderstorm) is coming from another. After sunset, on a clear day, usually around twenty minutes after the sun is gone, the sky will light up and provide a marvelous glow of diffused light, often colored if high clouds (cirrus or thunderstorms) are also present. Very special photographs can be made under such lighting circumstance. Be prepared to use a tripod.

TONE AND CONTRAST:

Tone is often thought of as being a darkroom thing, but we can use it in our outdoor photography by being aware of the range of tones present in our frame and setting the exposure to suit our needs. Photographers have developed a standard 11 step scale for measuring tone from white (0) to black (10). We might feel that we have a good photograph if it displays just 5 of those tone steps: 1) white, 2) light gray, 3) gray, 4) dark gray, and 5) black.

We always want to have a *"middle"* in our tonal range. If you have only dark and light, you will always be disappointed in the photo. If you can get a "middle" that would have at least one shade of gray, that would possibly give you a grimly acceptable photo. But, *if your "middle" can consist of three shades, plus dark and bright, your photo will probably appear to have **good tonal range**!*. Especially if it is a color print. What we are saying is that a photo with good tonal range will have a part of the picture that is dark (but still with detail in the dark), a part of it that is light (but still with detail in the light), a part that is in the middle, a part that is between the bright and middle, and a part that is between the dark and middle. Sometimes a "squint test" can help visualize the resulting photo; by squinting at the scene, you can often see if the scene "wants" to resolve itself into just a mess of brights and darks. Look at the photo in figure 4.1, it is typical of many photos shot at noon on a bright day.

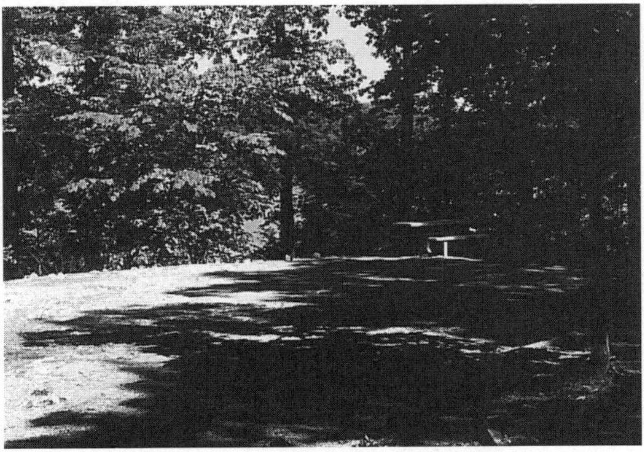

Figure 4.1. The Dark part is too dark, the Bright part is too bright, and the Middle is uninteresting. (But the exposure meter did a good job!)

How do you get more tones in your photo? First, by being aware of the opportunity and desirability. Second, by planning your shot with respect to the time of the day, the season, the lighting present at the time of the shot, selecting your view properly, and using good compositional discipline and sometimes, wild artistic abandon! Finally, the great shot that you know is here, may not be available today, or for six months. I have a "sketch" book where I write such information down. My day may come later! Figure 4.2 shows a photo with a more pleasing tonal range.

Basically, contrast is the degree of difference

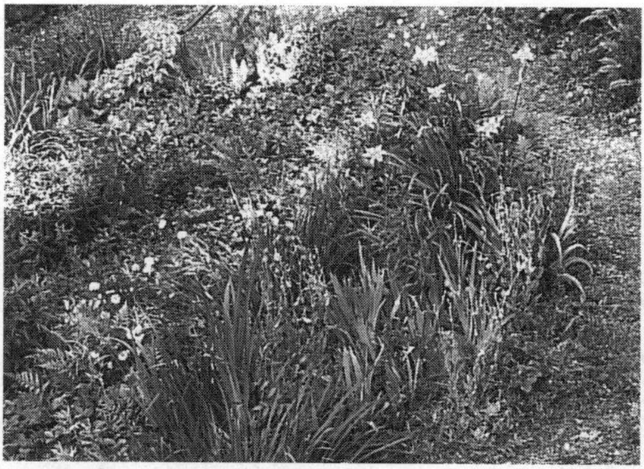

Figure 4.2. I can count seven tones in this photo..

between dark and light areas in a photo. Contrast is normally good, except when the difference between the light and dark areas are so great that your film cannot make an image that will show detail in either the light or dark, AND there is no middle range of tones. If the contrast range is great enough, there may be only two tones: too bright and too dark. Try a photo of a dark barn with a tin roof on a bright day about noon. You will get an extremely contrasty picture that looks like a dark smudge underneath a mirror. Figure 4.3 shows such a photo. It was made at noon on a deck in the summertime. If you look closely at the shadow of the table, you may be able to make out the shape of a black Labrador retriever. (His head is where 9:00 would be on a clock and his rump is about 1:00). It is common to find ourselves battling contrast this strong on any day with bright or filtered lighting between 10 a.m. and 3 p.m.

How can we handle contrast? Several methods can help. First, eliminate the contrast by framing so that you are concentrating only on either the light area or the dark area, but not both. When the photo shown in Figure 4.1 was made, if the photographer

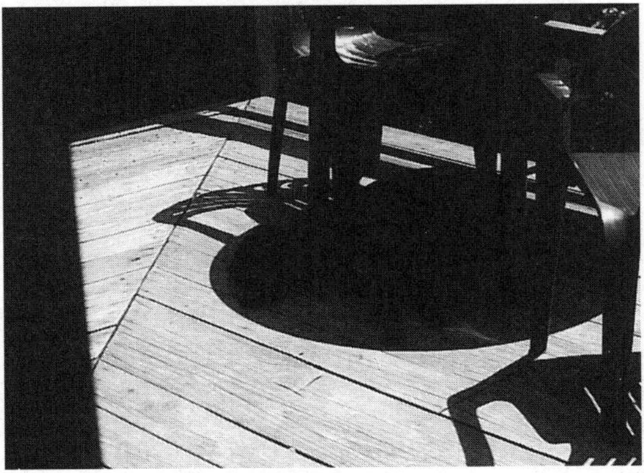

Figure 4.3. Contrast Problems. Again, the exposure meter did a good job!

had gone into the dark area and taken a reading and shot there, OR *kept* that reading that was made in the dark set in the camera settings and come back to the site of the shot, then a good photo could have been made of the dark area only. If you confine your photo to the dark area it will take on some of the aspects of filtered lighting so that it will have varying tones of intensity and directions as well as different color casts. Reflectors can also bring in a controlled amount of light from the sides. The bright areas can also be photographed by excluding the dark areas from your exposure readings. Neutral density or Polaroid filters, will almost certainly help and you may still need some shading. If the area in the bright light is small (such as a flower) it can be shaded by a cap or a photographer. When we photograph with a bright clear sun shining onto the object, we will want to try to soften that strong light.

Very strong contrast tends to lend a slightly macabre air of unreality to a photo. You might try something like that if your intention was to create a "protest" photograph of, say, garbage by the trail, or stream pollution, or clear-cutting, or mining. People who view the photo will immediately know something is wrong, even before they get the real message. **Contrast** can be *softened* by using *neutral density filters,* and *polarizing filters* can be useful in knocking out bright reflections.

TEXTURE

Texture is a measure of the complexity or smoothness of the objects in the photo. The art of photography often rests on the skill of the photographer to bring out texture in a subject; nothing else so effectively reveals the **fabric** of which the object is made. In the case of a portrait, texture will reveal not only skin and age, but also may tell something about character. **Shadows** can reveal texture, and also partly **faded colors** are effective. Texture can be *dramatically enhanced* if there are two or three contrasting forms of texture in the photo, arranged in a compositional format, such as rough and smooth surfaces, or grains that run in two different directions; or grain, pebbles, and smoothness. Figure 4.4 shows

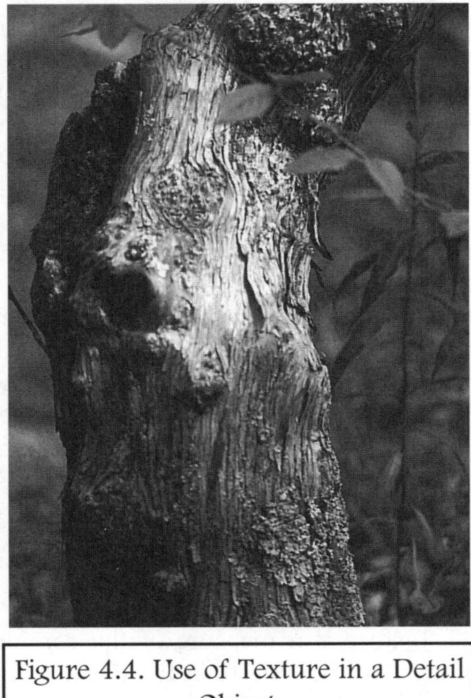

Figure 4.4. Use of Texture in a Detail Object.

texture taken from a tree trunk using sidelighting from an evening sun.

Texture can be assisted by using light reflectors. While photographic studio reflectors are expensive, cumbersome and poorly suited to travel in the mountain forests, discount stores often sell automobile windshield sun reflectors that have aluminum sides, for about $7 or so, and which fold up into circles small enough to fit into the back pocket of most vests. You can also sometimes find **natural reflectors** in the form of rock formations, water or snow, and clouds, especially thunderstorms.

Exposure Meter Modification.

The reason your exposure meter reading has to be modified is because it really doesn't know what it is reading or what you want in the way of a picture! *It has been rigged* to provide you with a setting that will produce a photograph of an average tone - that is to say, middle gray. This is surprisingly effective enough to get a lot of good photos, but only if you are shooting subjects that have an *average* tone or tonal range. The problem comes when you shoot a subject that is not a middle tone - such as white snow, or a black Labrador retriever. The exposure meter will give you a setting that will expose both of these subjects so they will look middle tone. The snow will be gray, the black Lab will be gray. So anytime you shoot a subject that is other than average tonal range, you will have to adjust your exposure setting. I do all of my serious shooting in manual mode. So I set my camera settings to the values given by the meter, and then adjust them according to how bright or dark the Subject is. My meter is trying to skew everything toward the middle, so if the Subject is dark, I will go darker (that is, take away light); if the Subject is bright, I will go brighter (that is, add more light)! What all this means is that I will let more light come in for bright Subjects and let less light come in for dark Subjects. How much do I change these settings? One increment of either shutter speed or aperture opening if the Subject is just light or dark, two if it is *very* light or *very* dark. See figures 4.5 and 4.6. Plate VI was was shot 1.5 EV

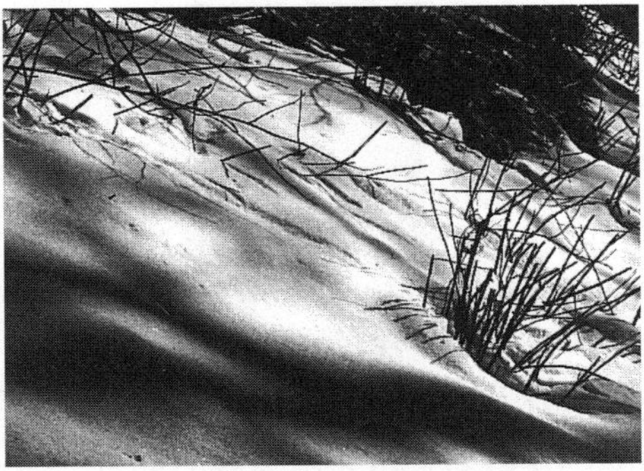

Figure 4.5.
Snow shot made with camera set on recommended exposure settings. The exposure meter has made the snow a middle-tone gray.

greater than the exposure reading: f/stop opened up one-half setting and shutter speed slowed one setting.

Remember - light is constantly changing, sometimes second-by-second there will be significant changes occurring in color, tone, tint, warmth, direction, brilliance, etc.

What about "bracketing"? Bracketing an exposure is more than just insurance. You might think that if you determine a shot should be made at

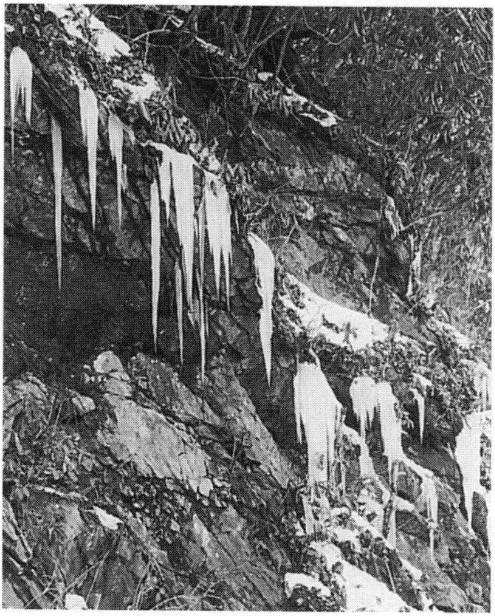

Figure 4.6
Snow shot with aperture opened up 1.5 f/stops beyond recommended reading has rendered the snow bright white.

a certain exposure, then if you make two more shots, one allowing more light into the camera and the other admitting less light, that you should get at least one good picture. I bracket my slide shots a lot, and often find that I get two good pictures, and they are usually the two that were bracketed while the one shot "right on" was not as good as the other two.

Bracketing your shots will also help to pick up any slack in performance in other factors. By that I mean that when you are shooting film rated at ISO 100, with f/4 aperture and 1/250 second, it may not be exactly as you think: 1) the film may *actually* be ISO 112, the aperture may *actually* be f/4.138, and the shutter speed may *actually* be 1/238 second. Also, there are nuances that are hard to read on the exposure meter, and the colorcast (color of the light that is present in the View or Scene) can affect the tonal qualities a bit. If I am aware that I may be shooting a "great" picture, I will always bracket. Bracketing is pretty much a slide photography thing. Some people recommend bracketing print film, but the only time I do that is when I am really not sure of the exposure setting.

Chapter Five

Color

First, a quick look at the color wheel. As outdoor photographers, we are not going to be concerned about the subtractive or additive properties of color, or primary or secondary colors. Why not? It's not because they are wrong - they are all very important to photographers, especially when you begin working with color photographs on computers. However, we need to carry all the information necessary to make photos with us, and we will have to use this information constantly with almost every composition and shot we make. So we will look at color a little differently.

Why be concerned with color anyway? The

paint artist, and the studio photographer can control their colors, but don't we just have to take what nature has given us? And we really can't change the colors we see, unless we use colored filters - and I do not suggest or recommend that! So we study color to find how to change that snapshot, with a mess of colors in it, into a really great photograph. Real estate salespeople will tell you about the usefulness of a red door, or even potted geraniums placed near the door, to attract the eye of the consumer, any advertiser spends a lot of money to make color work for them, and it is a tool we, as photographic artists, will use to grab the eye of the viewer, lead them into our photograph, and keep them there for a while. Some colors naturally fit well together and some don't; some combinations of colors attract the eye while others repel the same eye. And sometimes, while we can't change the colors we find, even a small effort to realign their relative relationships can make enormous changes in the colors we get in our photograph.

There appears to the human eye a certain natural harmony and disharmony among colors, perhaps deriving mathematically from their frequencies in the spectrum. We have all seen a prism cast its spectrum on a wall, and we have all studied the organization of colors as a color wheel, which tends to be difficult to remember for some of us, including the author. We will try a slightly different tack in this chapter.

Let's *see the color wheel as a clock*: Draw a circle that represents a clock. Inside the circle, up at the top, put a 12, for 12 o'clock - make the 12 a little sloppy. Put a 2 at 2 o'clock, 4 at 4 o'clock, 6 at 6 o'clock,

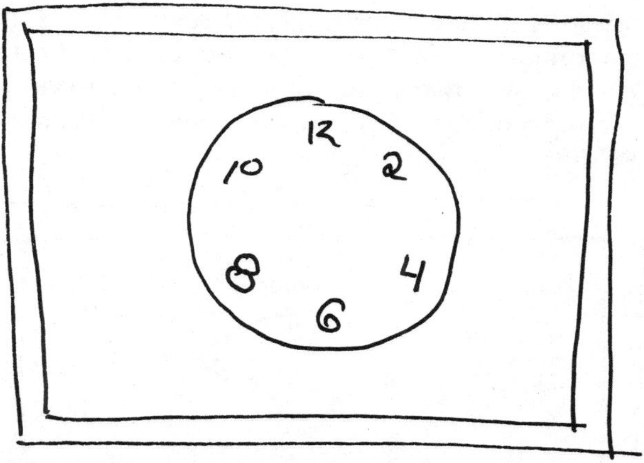

Figure 5.1.
The Color Clock.

8 at 8 o'clock, and 10 at 10 o'clock. Make all of these numbers "kinda sloppy" (that's important!). See Figure 5.1. Now go back on the outside of the "clock". Up at the top write "R" for red. Notice how the R looks like your "sloppy" 12. Now, at 2, write a wild "O" (for orange) and see a similarity there. At 4, write a "Y" and make it look like a 4. At 6, write a "G" for green, make it look like a 6. At 8, write a "B" for blue, see how a B can look like an 8. Then at 10 write a "P", make the P look like a 10. That's all you ever need to remember about the color wheel when you are shooting out in the real world.

We note that each color can be "pure", that it usually will have, or seem to have, **tints** of white or light gray, and **shades** of black or dark gray. "Red", for example, can appear as light pink or dark maroon, or anything "reddish" in between. So we might also see our color clock as having a virtually black hole in the center, and being surrounded on the outer limit by a large circle of tents, or tints of color. We also note that colors can flow together, so that varying amounts of yellow (4) and blue (8) can create different grades of green (6).

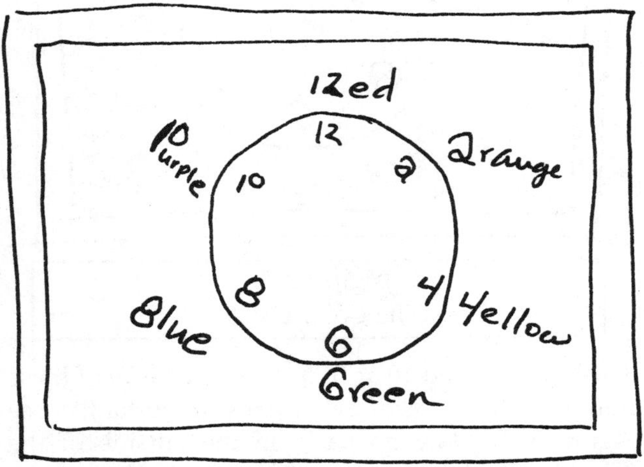

Figure 5.2 Color Clock with Colors.

How does this affect us as outdoor photographers? Well, we know already that certain colors seem to "go together" and others seem to "clash". Look at most houses in the typical sub-division: light blue paint, dark blue shutters, yellow trim, not bad - but then, what about the brown roof and red brick fence? Add green grass, a purple plum tree and a black asphalt driveway and you have a real challenge for any photographer. (you'd almost have to use black and white film!) Fortunately, though, since we are going to focus our cameras on the world of nature, a lot of our color harmony problem is solved at the beginning. So, let's look at some of the color schemes we will be working with.

1) One of the easiest color schemes to handle is the monochrome. A monochrome rendering would normally consist of three **shades** or **tints** of the same **hue**. We see it often in the higher mountains: the dark green of the firs, middle green of the beeches, and lighter greens of the wild grasses. Almost any view of a forest from a mountain will reveal different shades of green, and cloud shadows will often add spots of dark green to parts of the forest view. Monochrome composition can be easy to do, often requiring only maneuvering so that one or two colors are omitted from the frame, or that a lighter or darker aspect of the basic color is found and included.

2) The next scheme we will discuss is that of Color Harmony. Think of our mountainscape again, with its different shades of green; now, let's mix in a little blue from a small lake in the valley. (A polarizing filter may help you with this very dramatically!). A little blue from the sky may also fit in beautifully. What we have now, is a monochrome green color scheme with small amounts of blue for *accent*. Great! Looking back at the wheel, or clock, you can see that green (6:00) is "next" to blue (8:00), and they go "together" great. When they go "together" this well, we call that effect **color harmony**. So too, will any other "adjoining" colors on the clock harmonize with each other. In fact, we can propose a color harmony rule: That the colors of any Quadrant of our

Color Clock will fit together harmoniously. What about the "missing numbers": 1:00, 3:00, 5:00, etc.? Well, they are colors too, but are combinations of what is on either side of them. 1:00 might be called "reddish-orange", 3:00 might be called "brown", 5:00 could be called "yellow-green", 7:00 might be "teal", 9:00 could be "indigo", 11:00 could be "violet". At any rate, there are enough colors to go all the way around. The point here is that with all twelve numbers on the clock assigned to colors in this manner, *any three contiguous "hours" on the "clock" will tend to "go together"* ***harmoniously.***

3) The third scheme we will examine is that of Color Contrast. You can bring in a color on the other side of the "clock" IF it is not a large amount of color. In the basically green (6), and blue (8), mountain-lakescape we were just contemplating, a small, bright red (12) object (an airplane, say, or a flower) could be a magnificent touch because it would add a special dimension to the photo and would serve to heighten the beauty of the blues and greens; but it would have to be a very small part of the photo, probably about 5% of the total frame. This type of accent from the other side of the color clock is effective because it provides contrast to the color scheme of the photograph. Contrast can dramatically draw the eye of the viewer to (or in the direction of) items that the photographer wants to highlight. Contrast can also emphasize the harmony in the photo. Think back to a color scheme often used by old churches built in a Gothic-type style: usually the church has gray walls, with a little bit of white trim, and a lot of black wrought iron, and then look at the front door, and notice that it has been painted a brilliant red.

Doesn't that reach out and grab your eye, and practically drag you up to that door, and through it?

4) The fourth method of color combination discussed here is that of Color Balance. When you use three colors equidistant on the color clock, it would be advantageous to have the palest color occupy the greatest space in the photo and the brightest color use the smallest amount of space. Then the middle color, not pale nor bright, could be a bridge between the two. Let's say you wanted to photograph a yellow (4) hickory tree, next to a red (12) sourwood tree. These colors don't really go well together, so a photo of the two would seem to just be a mess of red and orange. What to do? Obviously, if you could bridge the gap, with a (2) orange, that might work, but if there is no orange present, then what can you do? Green (6) is present. Well, yes, but the color composition will not be balanced: with green, you would have 12, 4 and 6. But what about blue (8)? If you could get some bright blue sky (perhaps with the help of a polarizer filter), or some blue flowers (asters perhaps) you would have 12, 4 and 8. Balance would now be present! But before you shoot, what is the palest color? Yellow, of course, so I would try to let the yellow hickory leaves form the color cast of the photo. I would maneuver so that the photo will get a lot of blue in it, but not nearly as much as the paler yellow. Then, to complete the balance, I would bring in a few bright red sourwood leaves. Will people really notice the difference? Yes and no. Many of them will just say something like: "I like this picture, but I don't know why."

In a similar manner, green, blue and yellow could go well together, especially if the middle color, green in this case, were dominant, and the blue and yellow were small parts of the photo. See Plate IV, the blue of the sky is very small but very important. Alternatively, perhaps the color on one side, say green, (or yellow) could be clearly dominant, and then the middle color could occupy most of the rest of the photo, leaving the color on the other side to play the role of an accent. Try it and see if you like it. In the example in the last paragraph, when you were photographing the yellow (4) hickory leaves and red (12) sourwood, suppose that a bright orange (2) maple tree was close by! Now you have 12, 2, 4, and have harmony. I would try to make the middle color, orange in this case, the dominant color, and let the red and yellow come in as accents. If that didn't look like a good shot, then I might try to make red dominant, with the color on the other extreme (yellow or 4, here) a minor player in the photo, and let the middle (orange or 2) color bridge the gap.

So, we will generally try to keep one color dominant in the photo, and use other colors close to it on the color "clock" to bring in accents of harmony, or colors opposite from it on the color "clock" to introduce elements of contrast. The more two colors share in the photo, the closer on the color "clock" they should be to each other. Also, when using monochrome, one of the shades might be dominant and the others could play a supporting role.

Finally, don't forget the importance played by the use of Tone. Just because your color photo is not black and white doesn't mean that tone is not a very important part of your photograph. You will still want to try to get at least five tones in the photo. Granted that the light tone may be yellow-green, the middle tone may be blue, and the dark tone purple, with other tones supplied by other colors, but we still will need the tonal development in the photo.

Now, let's entertain the concept that there really is no such thing as absolute color, and that the color you see may not be the color that you get in the photo. It's easy to overrun the nuances of light and shade, and just see all trees as "green" and all sky as "blue". Take a moment and look closely at some trees. Pick one tree, and look closely at it. How many colors can you find on that one tree? Look for tints and shades, look at the effect of glare and shadow, see the colors of twigs and branches, and trunk, and any withered or "dead" leaves, are there any yellow, brown or yellow-green leaves? Why bother with all that? Well, it all shows up on the final photograph! Looking out my window, I can see leaves on a Black Oak, hanging in the shade that are virtually black, but I "see" them as green; two feet away, leaves on the same tree, backlighted by the sun, are brilliant yellow-green, and I also "see" them as green. Now, a cloud has covered the sun, and both sets of leaves are different than they were a moment ago. Now, they are dark green and light green, and as the cloud thickens, there is a uniform green color to both leaves. Others, on the other side of the same tree have a slight glare from the sky. My polarizing filter darkens that glare, but other leaves, facing the opposite side of the tree, pick up that glare. That's one part of one tree. And it's easy to look at it and say: "That's a green tree." And it is. But the photo will show all the black, yellow-green, green, and glare. And as a breeze picks up, all the colors, glints, glares and tints and shade go into motion. Watch the changing colors and lights carefully, see when they are flat, and when they are full of fire and life. Pick up the rhythm of the changing colors, shades, glints and glares; live with the tree and the light, and time your photo perfectly, and you may make an unforgettable image of an ordinary scene. (That may be what drove Van Gough over the edge!)

Colorcast is the background color tone of the area that is being photographed. It is the color of the light of the sky. It is the color of the air that you are shooting through. Usually it is faintly blue or yellowish. On some days it changes constantly, on others is is very stable. It is very easy to overlook, and once you have it pinned down, it can change before you are aware of it. Good watercolorists will pick up the *colorcast* of the scene or view they are looking at , and will choose a color pallet that is in harmony with the *colorcast,* and will mix and use only those colors. If Phalo Blue is one of those colors, then Ultramarine Blue will probably not be added, because if used in any other than a very small amount, the *colorcast* of the painting might begin to drift. As photographers, we are not going to mix colors on a pallet, but we will mix them on film. So *colorcast* analysis will be part of our Technical Composition, and it will be derived from our Interpretive Composition analysis. Often, in the mountain forests, the Colorcast will tend to be greenish or bluish or grayish. In the autumn that changes. Clouds that reflect color may change the colorcast, and it almost always changes at sunrise and sunset. The colorcast of a view may change from scene to scene, so if we are aware of colorcast nuances, and are looking for them, we can use them in our cropping before we shoot. The colorcast may not be noticeable, and then it can be overridden, but if you go with it, the photograph will look better.

The colorcast will change throughout the day. At dawn and dusk, **shadows** tend to be black. Objects seen against the sky appear as **silhouettes**. The light and color come from the dome of the sky, and can be good for photographic purposes for twenty minutes before sunrise and twenty minutes after sunset. If **clouds** are present, especially cirrus or thunderstorms, the light from the sky can be dramatic and even exotic when mixed with the light and colors reflected from the clouds. Dawn and dusk are also good times to try some photos under lighting conditions that your film was not made to handle, so very unusual results can occur. Make a picture with a small aperture and long exposure - let it silhouette mountains or trees - and you may get some very unusual skyscapes of magenta or a raspberry sky. Use a tripod and make exposures at maybe f/32 @ 3, 5, 10, 20 and 30 second shots. The colorcast may be magenta, or worse/better!

At sunrise and sunset, clouds will pick up the glow from the sun and **reflections** can brighten significantly. The sky will tend to become red, red-orange, or orange. **Shadows** will turn from black to blue as they pick up light from the sky. The general light background or colorcast will be more yellow. Sometimes a low cloud deck will flare into brilliance as the sunlight illuminates the under part of the clouds near the moment of sunset or sunrise. Usually, during the process of sunset/rise, there will come a fairly brief moment or two of brilliant light that engulfs the entire View or Scene in a fantastic glow of light and unearthly color tones. If you are waiting for it you will be able to photograph it. I am not saying to not shoot unless that brief period of lighting is present, go ahead and get shots; just be ready for the magic moments. They also happen through out the day.

Midday will bring truer colors, the shadows will tend to blacken again, and if there is a bright sun, **contrast**, texture and perspective can be serious problems. However, if we are in open shade, under a blue sky, the colorcast will be bluish. So your color pallet can be green, blue, yellow, or blue, teal, purple. A red object may look strange in the final photograph. If you are photographing a mountain stream under heavy trees, the colorcast will be greenish. Your pallet would be more green, yellow, blue. A small red object, a firepink flower, perhaps, might provide great contrast, but you wouldn't want much red in either of these two colorcast situations. What if you have a bluish colorcast from the sky, and want to include a brilliant yellow birch tree? You have a colorcast of blue (8), and leaves of yellow (4), so red (12) might fit O.K. The only problem then would be the mixture. You can try to make blue the background color, red the minor color, and let the yellow bridge the gap between blue and red.

During morning and afternoon, the light from the sky will tend to become more golden as the time varies from noon.

Darkness provides opportunities to make time exposures from the light of the moon. **Lightning** photos can be exposed with the lens open and the aperture set to your smallest setting; leave the lens open for several strokes.

Weather changes can enhance almost all photography. An overcast can eliminate the blue of the sky and yellow from the sunlight. An overcast will tend to enhance **autumn** foliage shots, and will also bring out the true green of leaves and grass. Cloud glow, especially from cirrus or thunderstorms can provide a different view of familiar places.

Painters often mix different color schemes into one painting. Look at figure 5.3. You will see five different areas, all of them fitting into basic compositional arrangements, but it is possible that each of the areas could have their own color scheme. Area 4, for example, could show oranges, reds and yellows; 5 could be a green monochrome, with some yellow-green and perhaps some blue shadows; 3 might be a field of flowers, with reds and yellows and perhaps some blue; 1 and 2 could highlight blues, purples and lavender.

So, that would be a "busy" painting, you're right - *very* busy! But it demonstrates a point of not feeling restricted to just one color scheme for each photo. You probably won't be looking for five dif-

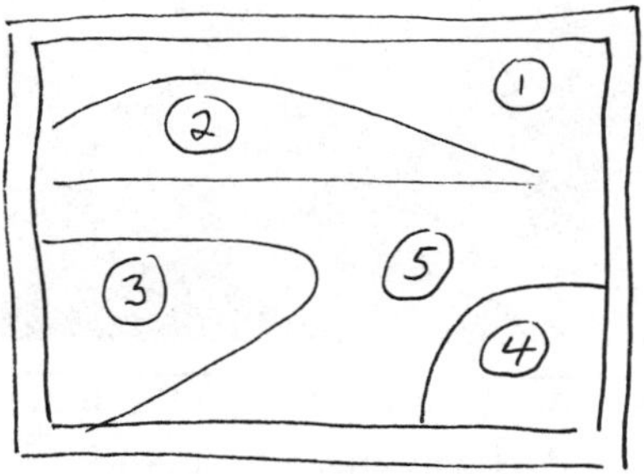

Figure 5.3. Many color patterns.

ferent color areas, but you might very well bring two (and occasionally even three) into some photos. To see this kind of work done by masters, see the book *Provence,* with photos by Sonja Bullaty & Angelo Lomeo.

What do you do if you see a beautiful Scene and its colors don't match any of the color schemes we discussed? I go ahead and shoot them and know that I am in the presence of a master artist who is showing me something I don't understand yet.

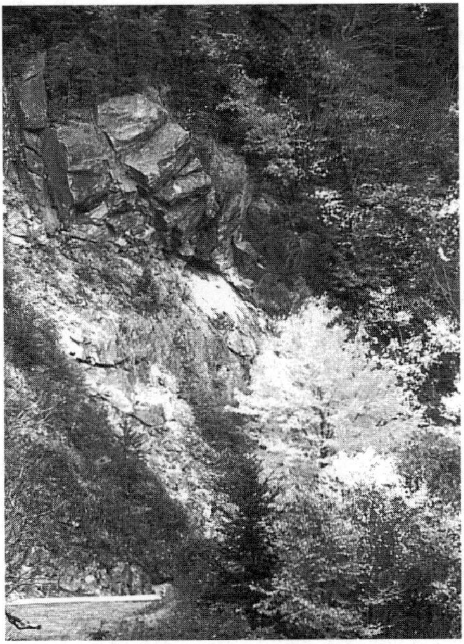

Figure 5.4. Autumn day on the Blue Ridge Parkway near mile 448.

Chapter Six

Mountains, Landscapes and Skyscapes

Mountains are not easy to photograph, partly because they seem a lot taller to us when we regard their regal presence thrusting up into the sky, than they do on a piece of photographic paper that is 3 inches wide. It is not the amount of vertical feet they rise that counts, it is the **number of angular degrees** they occupy in the photo. It's like shooting the moon with a 50mm lens. No matter how big the moon looked at the time of the shoot, it still only occupies about one angular degree in the sky, which is only 1/180th of the visible dome of the sky, and only 1/50th of the frame. There are some techniques we can use to help accentuate the mountain landscapes, and a few are suggested in the passages that follow. All of them work well, but not all of them will be effective on any given day. Lighting, contrast, haze, weather, sightseers, seasonal colors, and many other factors contribute to specific technique selection. There are some techniques that can help enhance our mountain photos, and some suggestions follow.

1) Most importantly, we can use the mountain horizon as a modifying element that is present in photos that present other Subjects or Objects. The mountain horizon, photographed from six to ten

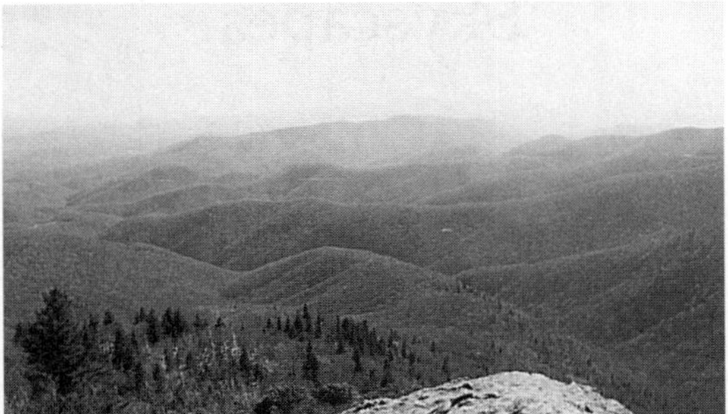

Figure 6.1. The mountain environment with foreground, a middle, and many ridgelines.

miles away, will usually not be dramatic unless it can be significantly enlarged. Smaller peaks or ridges can be very dramatic if they are photographed from less than a mile distance. A good way to show the distant mountain horizon is in a "Mountain Environment" out there in the distance behind a closer peak, a great tree, large boulder, or some other primary Object. See figure 6.1 for an example of this. Even at sunset/rise, there is still the need for a near-by Object. If you make a photo with a tree branch dominating 75% of the photo with a small view of the distant mountain horizon visible underneath the branch, the mountain horizon will seem to stand out dramatically.

2) Another technique concerns the placement of the mountain horizon. We have previously said that horizons should normally be placed in either the upper or lower third of the frame. That is general information, that will consistently yield good photos. However, there are two more options that I often consider when composing, and let me discuss them here. They concern placing the horizon at the very top of the frame and in the center of the frame. My decision turns on the type of picture I want to obtain, and often I will use more than one of these options, that is I will make several shots of a good Scene, and sometimes I will relocate the horizon in different parts of the frame on different shots. I usually put the horizon in the a) lower third, when the sky is very dramatic, or when I want to emphasize a feeling of loneliness associated with the top. Sometimes I place the horizon in b) the center when the picture is made from a high area looking out over land that is lower that the site of the view. The sky must be somewhat photogenic in order to do this, although this type of placement can be very effective

when the ground and sky merge in some unseen area and you look at the picture not sure *where* the horizon actually is. These pictures can covey a sense of vastness, however they seem to require either a substantial Subject be placed in the lower part of the frame or a dominant Object such as a tree or boulder that spans virtually the entire vertical frame; otherwise, there will be no picture. See Plate III. I tend to place the horizon in c) the upper third when the sky is very photogenic (that is, very blue, or with great thunderclouds, or perhaps a dark menacing cloud that lurks behind the horizon), and often use this placement for fairly short range photographs that usually focus on a feature on the side of the mountain, such as shadows, colored leaves, cliffs, etc.. Perhaps most often I simply place the horizon at d) the very top of the frame when I want to present the mountain itself. This is almost a necessity when the sky has a milky white overcast to it; then, if I show the sky at all, it will be just a small area of white at the upper edge of the frame and will only serve to outline the shape of the mountain ridges. When I use the d) method, I will be careful to set the exposure from a reading taken from the mountain and NOT from any part of the sky that may be seen in the photo. If the sky is not appealing, I do not want it in the frame.

3) Another method is to span a great valley such as one can see from the top of Albert Mountain in North Carolina, looking east toward the Fishhawk Mountains. That view is especially indicative of mountainscape photography because of the valley and also, at sunrise(set) there are those long, long shadows that reach out for miles. Detail will get lost

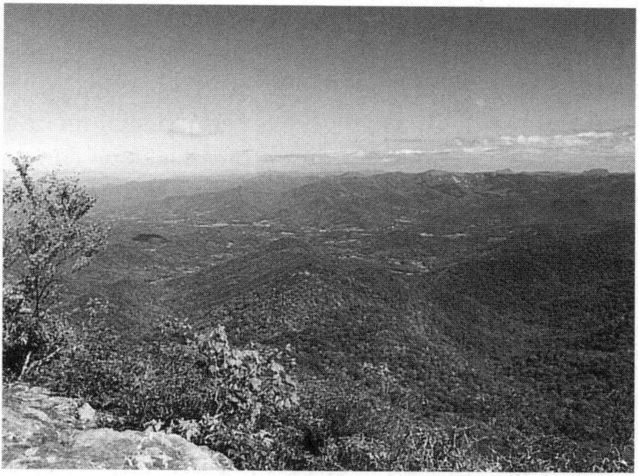

Figure 6.2. Franklin, N.C. viewed from Picken's Nose.

in these photos, and I like to use wide angle lenses and try to get something that is obviously part of the mountains (boulder, fir tree, hemlock, ledge, colored leaves in the autumn) clearly in the foreground, then let the vast distance sweep on out. Figure 6.2 shows such a view from Picken's Nose, on the Georgia-North Carolina border, looking out over Franklin, N.C.

4) Distortion. Long lenses tend to compress the elements present in the photo. This can either destroy the feeling of distance or enhance it. Sometimes, it seems to completely eliminate space and replace it with another dimension, the dimension of time, especially when you have photographed a mountain moonrise at six power magnification or greater. Short lenses can give a great

depth of field, and can bring perspective to an amazing new level if a very nearby object is positioned in one corner of a wide-angle photo that sweeps out into infinity. This can easily be overdone, but pictures made like this can give a very special feeling of the location, because so much of it is seen. The various items seen in such a shot though should be well composed. In the autumn, this can be very effective when composing, say, nearby blue aster flowers with a mid-range hemlock, and a very tall maple that is ablaze with golden leaves. In this case, every thing in the photo from the nearest flower to the top leaf of the maple would be in focus, and each object would occupy close to 1/3 of the frame. (And a single Oswego Tea, adding its bright red color over in a cor-

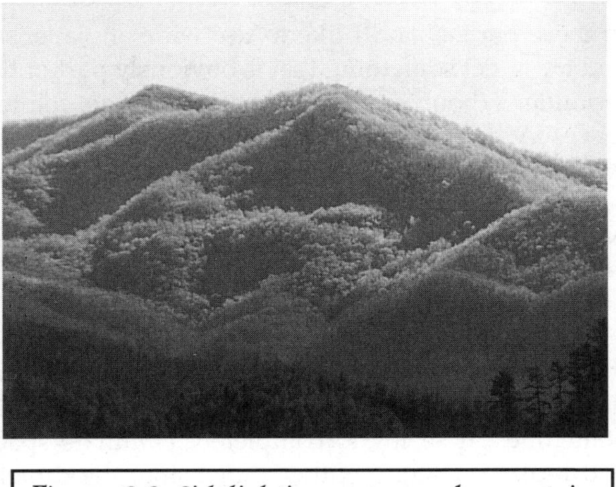

Figure 6.3. Sidelighting can reveal mountain ridges dramatically as this snowy day shows. From Wayah Bald, Macon Co. N.C.

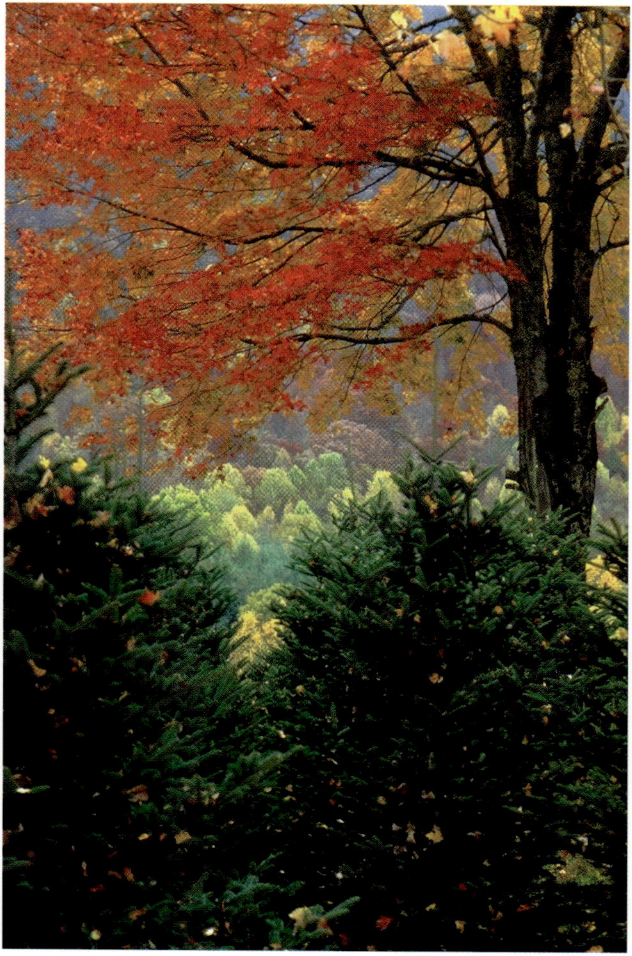

Plate I

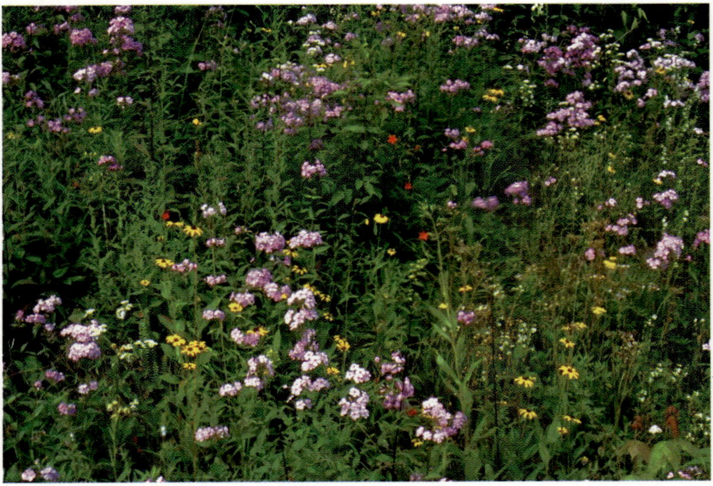

Plate II

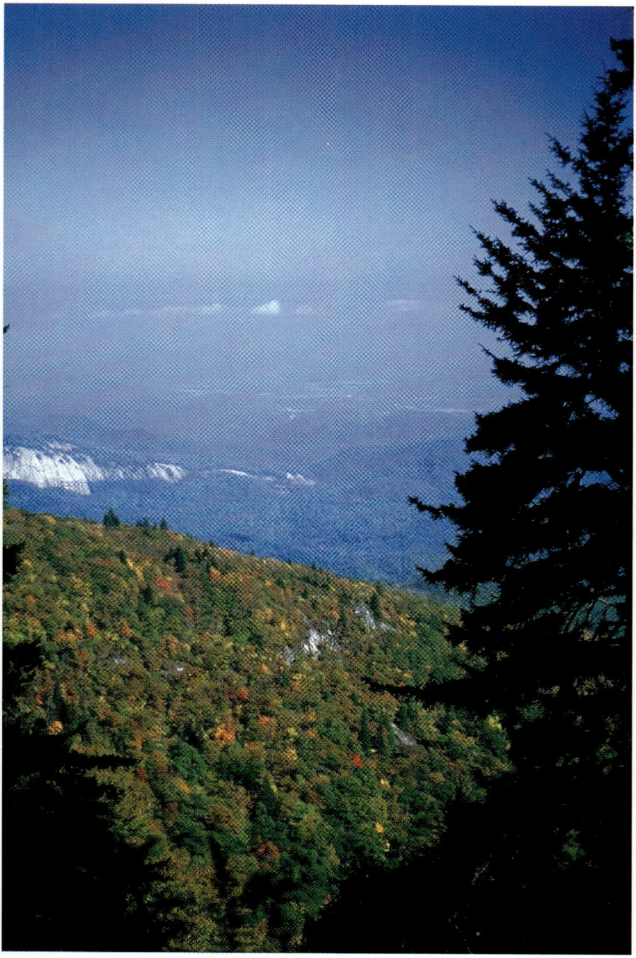

Plate III

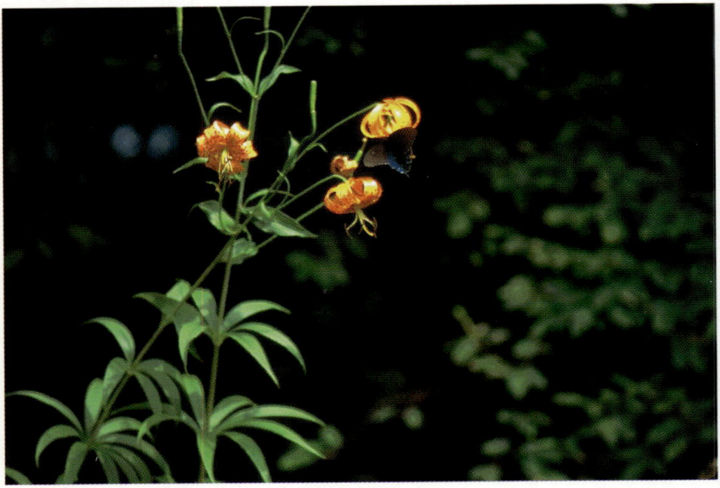

Plate IV

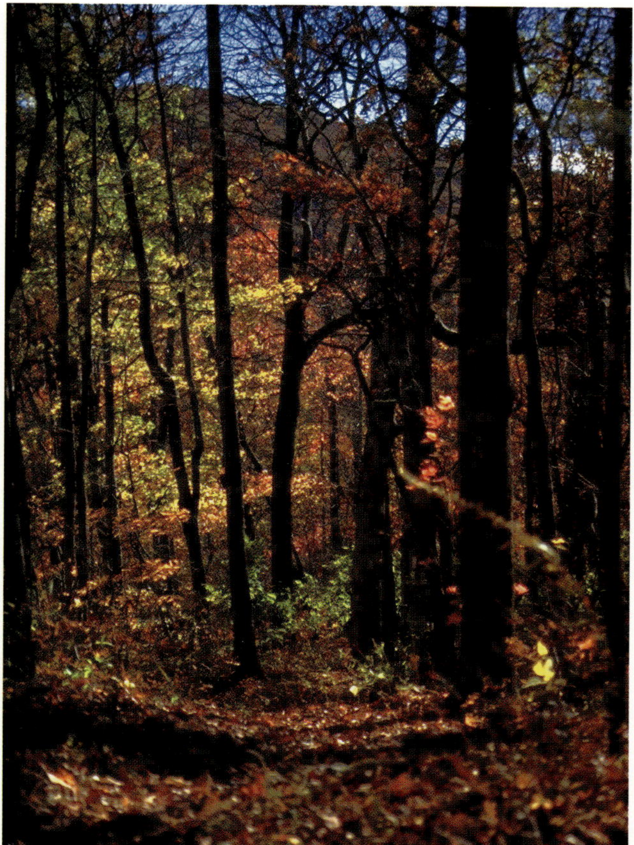

Plate V

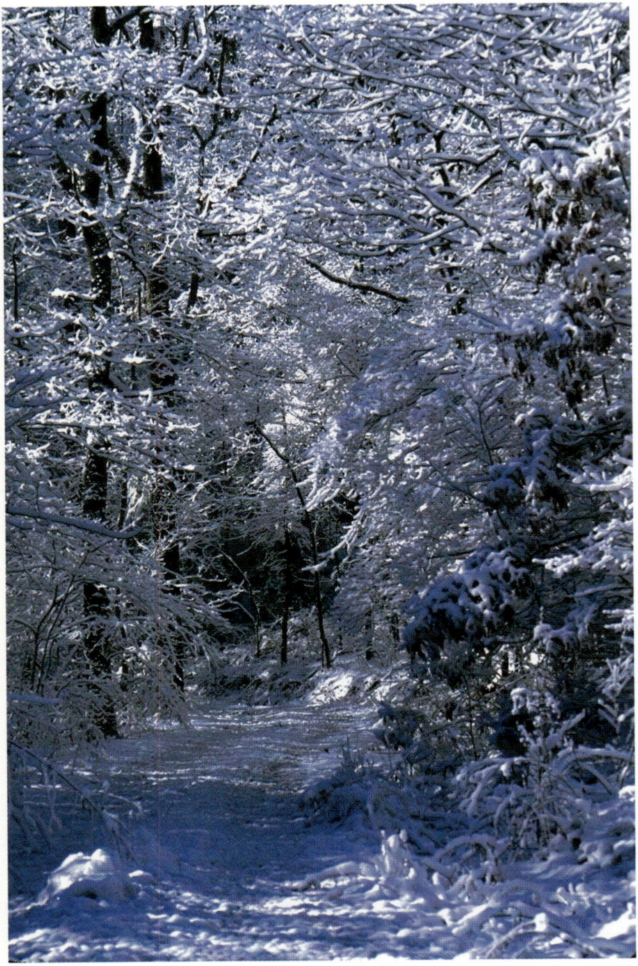

Plate VI

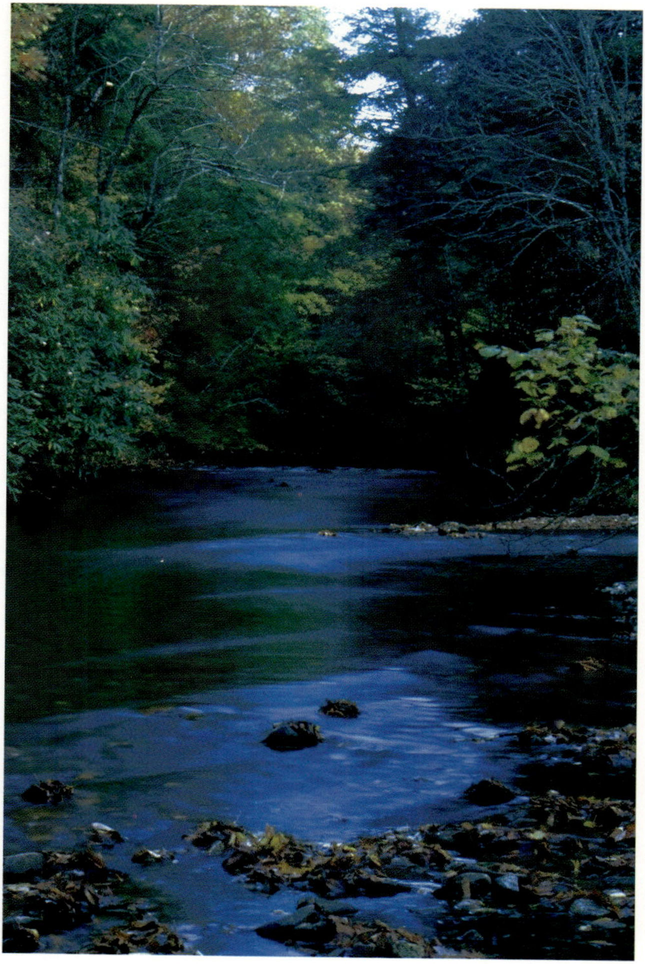

Plate VII

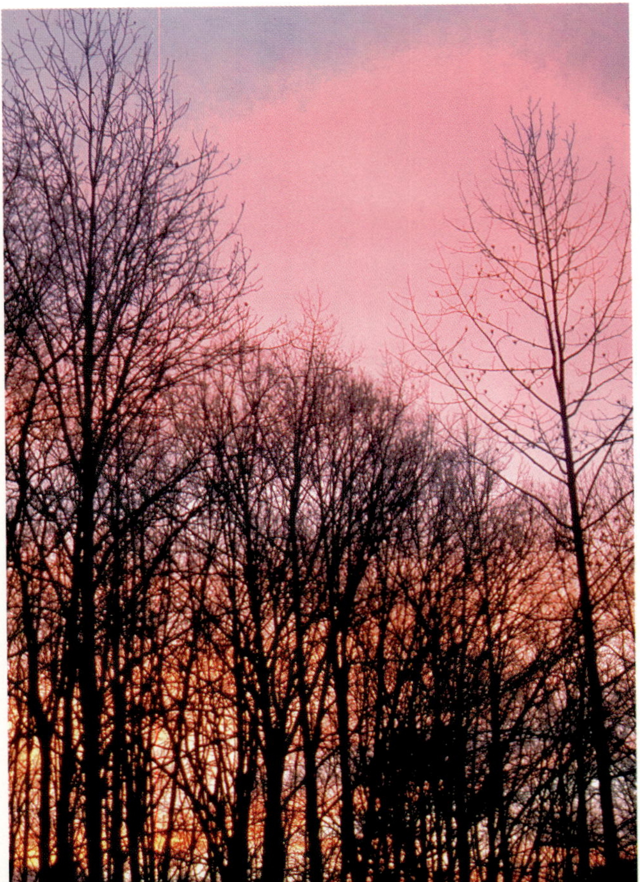

Plate VIII

ner could add a brilliant touch of contrast!)

5) Lighting is always a problem in landscape photography. You pretty well have to take what is given. **Sidelighting** can help very much. See figure 6.3. **Backlighting** usually doesn't do much for landscapes. Light from **behind the photographer** will give you a flat 2-D photo, and the worst of all are the **high noon** pictures; they can get close to 1-D. Shadows will be a good friend when you are making photos of mountains. Some kind of side lighting which is about 45° on either side of a line which is 90° from the photographer to the subject will produce good shadows. And the sun should be within 45° to 50° between the horizon and the zenith. Cloud shadows on the mountains may be able to help significantly. (see figure 6.3) Landscapes are hard to do properly between 10 a.m. and 2 p.m. or between 10 a.m. and 3 p.m. during daylight saving. Please refer to appendix B concerning the sun at 45 degrees.

6) Use perspective to help create the illusion of a third dimension. Some techniques that are often effective for this are listed in the section that follows.

PERSPECTIVE.

1) Convergence of parallel lines. We all know the image of the railroad tracks reaching across the desert, slowly joining each other in the far distance. This is a case of ***solo convergence,*** that of the tracks alone, and that is very effective in providing a feeling of depth and great distance. If there are telephone poles beside the tracks, or anything else that can provide another set of converging parallel lines, we have a ***reinforced convergence***. This can be

used with many features found in the outdoors. Valleys, lakes and even mountains can be used. At sunrise and sunset, the mountain shadows that reach across to the horizon are effective. Don't overlook the impact that a rather small item, such as an angled rock, or a leaning tree, or a close ridgeline can add to the perspective of a photo. Almost any mountain photo ever made has something like this that is already right there at the site.

2) Diminishing scale is another technique for introducing perspective. In this case, several similar objects are seen at different distances from the camera. To be effective, the relative sizes of the objects must be apparent. A version of diminishing scale is the use of **overlapping objects**, one behind the other, leading the observer's eye into the photo. Cityscapes often use this method by overlapping rooftops one behind the other, leading the eye far out to another scene. This is often accomplished in the mountains with those sunset photos of ridgelines standing one behind the other leading out to the sun itself. Sometimes we see photographers using rocks in a stream, or trees overlapping one another as they (the rocks or trees) lose their individual identity in the distance.

3) Multiple Horizons. Often, good mountain photographs take advantage of multiple horizons. Normally, we think of the horizon as being the ultimate separation between earth and sky. In mountain photography, I try to consider an intermediate horizon being *any* threshold that your vision must cross as you look out across the view, scene or into a photo. There may be a rocky outcropping fifty feet away that could be called your first horizon.

Then a ridge line could be the second horizon. Another ridge coming down from another direction could be horizon number three; a gap behind that could be number four, then there might be a higher ridge behind that, and behind it another. Figure 6.1 is an example of this type of multiple horizons. Maybe even a beautiful cloud layer could function as yet another. All of these horizons will lead the eye of the imagination outward treating the viewers to a feast of different textures, colors, tones, all of which introduce perspective into your photograph as a third dimension. In the mountains, there is seldom a lack of multiple horizons. What there is often serious lack of is multiple horizons that will photograph well. In order to make the most of multiple horizons, you will need shadows, either of clouds or those characteristic of a setting/rising sun. Get the shadows so they highlight one ridge in darkness while the one in front and behind it is light. This takes a lot of time, but good art is timeless. Poor pictures require a lot of explanation; great photos leave everyone speechless.

4) A form of perspective that is often called "Aerial Perspective" is the use of atmospheric conditions to provide the feeling of depth. We have a lot of *aerial perspective* in the Blue Ridge Mountains in the summer! In fact, one of the main problem we experience then is trying to avoid it, or to use it "creatively" by tying the mist into a mystical or mysterious aspect. Haze and fog, mist, rain, or clouds can sometimes help with this. While the constant haze can frustrate photographers not familiar with these mountains, it is almost a defining characteristic of our summer. The haze is often caused by hydrocar-

bon particles and water vapor released by the great mountain forests, and unless there is a wind sweeping across the ranges, each peak and valley tends to manufacture its own weather, and then these various micro-climates slowly mix and re-form. Air in the valleys will warm up and rise. As they reach the tops of the mountains, they condense into clouds. Then they rest, become cooler, and descend back into the valley again, or into the next valley, because they are now heavier due to the condensation. As they descend, they force warmer air up out of the valleys which will condense as they rise, hence the slowly rising wraith-like specters of "smoke" that are so common here. Those are distinguishing marks of the Smokies (although I have seen them in the Rockies, Sierra Nevada, and Yellowstone National Park.) They can help add dimension, perspective and

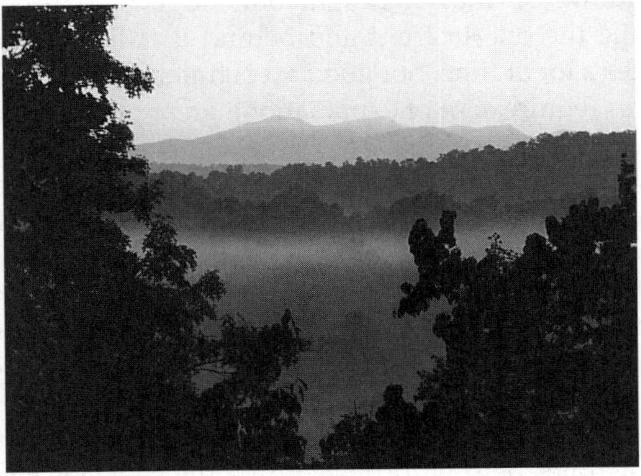

Figure 6.4. Clouds used for perspective.

mood to some of the photos made here. Figure 6.4 is an example of using clouds for perspective.

Some filters can help, but not much. Haze, UV, and Skylight filters can provide a small amount of enhancement; they don't "penetrate" anything, but can help remove a little blue from cloudy and hazy views. Polarizing filters can darken blue skies if the sun is in the proper location. A blue filter can help to intensify fog, mist or clouds (as if we need that here!) Infrared film won't help; it is at its best in clear weather conditions. Probably your best bet in haze and fog is to try to get some shadows, and see if you can find any side lighting. Again, if you have haze and fog, you may have to let the landscape shots go; but you don't have to quit making photos! Think of how a mountain creek or lake can become part of a magic kingdom with a little mysterious fog - and how about some tree-shape silhouettes?

5) Perspective can often be brought into the photograph through the careful use of color. We have studied how to select color mixtures in chapter five, and when we are setting up our shot, we can also remember that "warm" colors tend to advance toward the observer and "cool" colors tend to recede. If closer objects are red, say, and background objects are blue, such as one often encounters in the mountains in autumn, the depth perception will be enhanced by the colors. If the blue objects are closer and the red objects are farther away (such as often happens in sunrise and sunset photos), the colors can diminish the effect of perspective. In this case, you have a few choices: You can a) go with a two dimensional aspect, just getting sunset and mountains, and emphasizing whichever one you desire.

b) You can introduce a mid-point object, such as a ridgeline or a tree that rises out of the mountains and above the sun. c) You can bring in some convergence views, solo or reinforced, if you can find any.

6) Tilt. Perspective can play strange tricks when you tilt your camera up or down to make a photo of a tall object because the resulting perspective will make the vertical lines in the object appear to converge or diverge. This can make a tall building or cliff look like it's falling over backward. Not much can be done with this, (unless you have a view camera) and it's not all bad; sometimes your photo is just perfect with this distortion present. It can be eliminated by making a level lens shot (meaning a long way away). It may be used more effectively by making the highest point of the object occupy the top center of the photo frame

SKYSCAPES

Now, what about skyscapes? Well, you really can't get away from them if you plan to shoot landscapes. The main problem with the sky is that it can throw an enormous amount of light into the frame and wash out everything else. A beautiful clear sky can be photographed by simply metering it. But, a washed out, milky-white sky is probably not going to photograph at all. Great swirls of cirrus clouds floating like lace in a deep blue sky can photograph well, but are meaningless unless there is some ground provided in the photo for perspective. Nice shots can be made of such a sky when looking up toward the summit of a rise, and placing the horizon in the lower third of the frame. The sky can usually be metered straight. Just take a reading from the View, set the readings into the camera and shoot.

Ask most people about sky photos, and they often think of sunset and sunrise pictures. Sunrise and sunset photos will usually be more effective if you hide the sun, at least partially, from the lens (perhaps by a tree trunk, or tree limb or rock or rise of ground, or something like that - clouds are also good for this), so you don't make a picture of the SUN rising, but of the sunRISE atmosphere. See figure 6.5. Or, you could take a reading from the brightest area, then stop down one or two EV. Is there any difference between the two? After all, the sun is at the same angle to the sky and earth whether it is morning or evening. That's true, but there are subtle differences. There is often less pollution in the lower

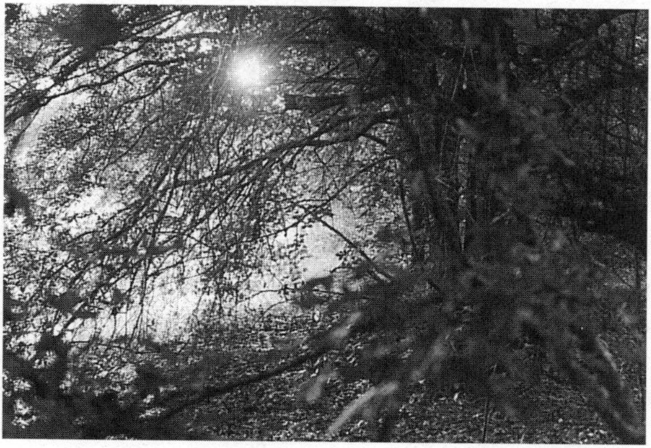

Figure 6.5. Sunrise with sun partly hidden by tree.

part of the sky in the morning; human activity is usually greater in the evening. The morning sometimes has dew or frost present in contrast to the evening. Daylight creatures of the woods are usually more visible in the morning than are the creatures of the night; as evening dusk approaches, the opposite is true. There are often significant differences in clouds that are present at sunrise and at sunset due to the probability that the earth has been heated throughout the day and cooled in the night. Thunderstorms are generally creatures of the evening rather than the morning, although on the beach, that may be reversed. When the mountains are in late autumn or spring, orthographic lifting, as fronts move through, can cause thunderstorms at any time.

Phenomena often accompany sunrise and sunset, and are usually overlooked by photographers, but, if you are looking for them you can find and photograph them, often with pleasing results. Discussion of such phenomena probably go beyond basic photography but would include such occurrences as *Crepuscular Rays, Iridescence, Coronas, Sun Pillars, Parhelia*s (commonly called "Sun Dogs"), and of course, *Haloes, Arcs, Subsuns, and Rainbows. Crepuscular Rays* appear to fan out (although they really don't) and can turn a beautiful sunset(rise) into a fantastic one. How do you meter these phenomena? Probably direct metering of the sky, and clouds, then taking the lower reading will produce an effective photo - and don't forget to bracket your exposures.

Clouds are too often taken for granted when we talk about skyscapes. Many beautiful cloud photographs have been made of clouds with silver linings and gold linings. Reflected light from clouds at sunset/rise can be fantastic, and cloud shadows can shade other clouds. Don't forget that sunsets/rises are a View, thus very hard to photograph. Try the grand view of the whole event, by all means, but also find a good Scene or two, and make some *great* pictures! See Plate VIII for a sunset colorcast photo.

One area I won't say much about, but which is sometimes used by slide shooters, is that of making sandwich slides. In this circumstance, two slide mounts are opened, the slides are removed and then mounted together, one on top of the other, in another slide mount. Think of how spectacular a great flaming red sunset slide would look if it were mated with an absolutely black silhouette of trees, or a slide with a mountain ridgeline in the background. This is an old procedure that is coming back with great gusto in the form of computer digital manipulation.

For silhouettes, meter from the brightest part of the sky and use as is. Try to shoot with an aperture of f/16 or smaller; this will often require a tripod, but will greatly improve your photos because the resulting photos will be much clearer with a greater field of view and they will sometimes pick up a special sparkle. The black part of a silhouette must be absolutely black. Try it and see what you think. Figure 2.9 shows such a silhouette.

Some interesting photographs can be made simply by shutting the aperture setting to the smallest possible, and also bringing the shutter speed down to a very slow setting. This will require time exposures, and will also require the use of a tripod. A generally accepted rule of thumb is that we should not expect to get a reliable handheld photograph when our shutter speed is lower than the focal length we are using. If we use a 50mm lens, we should be able to shoot hand-held shots at or faster than 1/50th second. If we are using a 70 - 210mm zoom lens, then we could expect to probably get reliably well focused shots at 1/60th second when the lens is set at 70mm, but when you zoom out to 210mm, then you will probably not want to shoot a hand-held shot at less than about 1/250th second. Wind effect can make this problem worse. If you don't have a tripod, you can improve your chances by bracing your camera against a tree or setting it on a rock or log. Some photographers carry a small bean bag just for this purpose. They will place the bean bag on a log or rock, then securely position the camera on the bag. Even when you have taken precautions such as this, there remains the likelihood that when you press and release your shutter, that will probably introduce motion into your camera and cause a blurring of the final photo. (Remember, it doesn't take enough blurring to be apparent. It only takes enough to kill the sharpness, to detract from a really good photo.) This problem can be avoided by using a cable release which will handle your shutter operation with virtually no camera movement. Cable releases are generally inexpensive, and can either operate the shutter with a push-release action, or can be locked into the open position to allow for longer time exposures. If you don't have a cable release, you can accomplish the same task if your camera has a self-timer mode. I have never bought a cable release for my Nikon, so I use the self-timer, usually leaving it set on about five seconds, and then using that to operate the shutter with virtually no camera movement at all.

Chapter Seven

Flowers and Detail Objects

Perhaps the best thing about photographing flowers is that the flower can continue to live as a flower while it also can live as a work of art. A picked flower will seldom last more than one week, while a good photograph can last for many years. Many of our wildflowers are on the Endangered Species List, and others are in very short supply and great demand. They have a good bit of work to do, and flowers do produce seeds which are necessary to continue the species. If a flower is picked at the wrong time, there will be no seeds. So the first rule of photographing wildflowers is to take only the picture, not the flower. If you would like to duplicate the flower, return at the appropriate time for seeds, and then remember to scatter at least half of the seeds at the site of the flower. (Better yet, rough up the ground with your boot, put seeds in contact with the earth and gently press down with your foot. Then gently cover with leaves. Most wildflower seeds that do not germinate fail because they are buried too deeply.) Seeds can usually be taken in adequate number from roadsides. If construction is scheduled for a site with a good display of flowers, get permission, then get transplants. And don't forget the photos!

Basic props for detail photography are reflectors, shades, tripod, background cloth, and a "black box". The "**black box**" is simply a large (say, 2 foot by 2 foot) cardboard box that has had its interior spray- painted flat black. It will be placed behind the flower, and the photo will be made of the flower against the interior of the box. This will help the flower to stand out clearly, and is extremely effective when making photos for use in identifica-

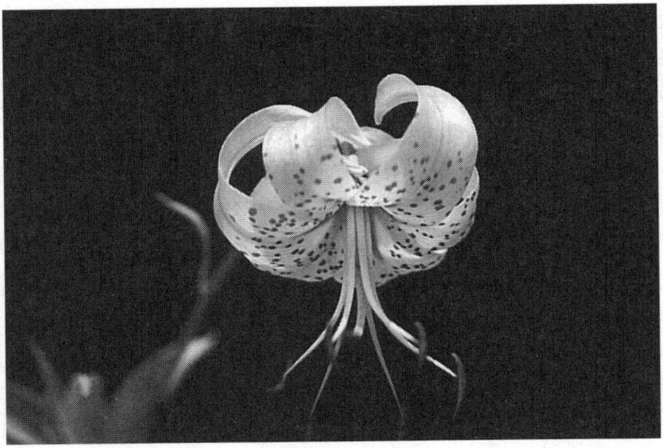

Figure 7.1. "Black-box type" photo of Carolina Lily (*Lilium michauxii*)

tion books, so all parts of the flower (calyx, petals, sepals, corollas, bracts, etc.) can be clearly seen. See figure 7.1 for an example. A piece of cloth could also be used to provide background for the object, and shade can be provided by many objects such as **background cloth**, a reflector (which is not reflecting), a companion, or even the photographer. Light can be thrown onto the flower with a **reflector**, a mirror, or anything shiny. Many people don't like a photo that has a flower against a black background. So your "black box" could be painted dark blue, green, brown, green-brown, "cammo", etc. Of course, as figure 7.2 shows, you can also shoot the flowers in their native habitat.

The main problems in flower and detail photography concern **lighting**, **background**, and **wind**. The best lighting is natural sunlight, whether direct, reflected or diffuse. One of the great advantages of

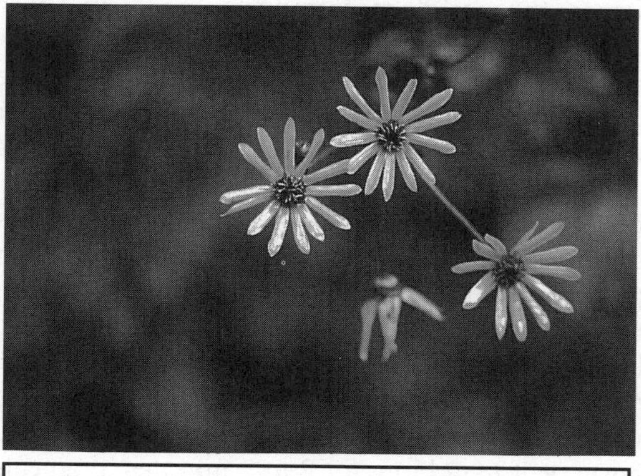

Figure 7.2. Young Woodland Sunflower (*Helianthus divaricatus*) Photographed in a natural environment.

reflected sunlight is that the different angles which can be available allow light to be directed to the most effective area of the frame. I will often shade the flower from direct sunlight with one reflector, then use another reflector to bounce light in from a low side angle to help bring out texture, tone, color and dimension. Flash is very effective for shooting at a fast shutter speed, which can help eliminate the background, especially if you have TTL flash capability. If you have a synchro cord for your flash, you can also use side lighting, or bounce lighting. Sometimes flash is the only way one can make wildflower photos if the day is windy.

Backgrounds can be enhanced if you do a little "gardening"; look for items that will become distractions in the photo and remove them. Real outdoor photographers will respect the presence of other vegetation just like they do the wildflowers. Many of the world's most important medicinal herbs are commonly called "weeds", and "weeds" are an important source of food and shelter to many species of wildlife. So we will **tie** these back, or obscure them from the subject and its elements whenever possible. Here's where the background **cloth** or "**black box**" can come in very handy. You can also use **sticks and stones** to hold flowers from swaying or to support the cloth. Also notice what pattern the wind is forming when it blows. Usually, it will be blowing in waves and **cycles** somewhat like waves at a beach. The wind may gust once or twice each minute, blowing for 15 or 30 seconds or so, and then pause; or it may blow for 2 to 3 minutes, then calm for a few moments, and then repeat. Or it may blow more or less constantly with occasional brief lulls.

See if you can find the cycle in the wind and use that to prepare for photography in the calm periods. Actually, being aware of the wind cycles and how they change from one into another as each day progresses should become one of the skills that an enthusiastic hiker will want to develop.

Lighting is often the key to flower photography. We have already discussed how the natural light can either come from above or to one side of the object, or how it can light up the front of the object, or how it can come from behind the object, providing what we call **backlighting.** With objects like tree trunks and rocks, a strong **side light**, or 45° overhead lighting angle, will bring out texture, and also provide a 3-D effect helping to separate the object from its background. Flowers also tend to benefit from sidelighting and 45° **overhead lighting**. Remember! Kill the glare that might show up on the petal parts or leaves. With flowers, the proper lighting can show all the parts of the flower and help bring out the range of colors found in the sepals, petals, stamen, pistils and anthers, etc. **Shadows** are particularly helpful in showing the shape of the leaves. Some of the most dramatic lighting for autumn leaves, is obtained with **backlighting**. Keep the brilliance of the sun and sky out of the frame, and just let the leaf be lighted with the sun shining through it. Some of the most dramatic lighting for flowers is also backlighting that lights the flower up like a flower light bulb! This also provides a great opportunity to compose a photo with a bright red (or yellow) leaf in one corner of the photo, which will lead the eye into the darkness of the forest, or into a slightly out-of-focus view of the mountains out in the distance. But if the sun is in, or near the frame, then the entire picture changes. Finally, don't forget to reflect light onto the subject. See how that changes the effect of your subject. If it helps, try a shot, and see what kind of a photo that makes. Good exercise: Get a tree in full autumn foliage, and shoot it from all sides. If the sun is coming from behind the photographer, you can work other colors in; if it is coming from the side, you can bring in some sky (dynamite with polarizing filter!); then, use back-lighting to light up the tree. Later, compare them.

Visualize before you shoot. Take a moment and ask yourself **why** you intend to shoot this one object and not others - **what** was the main thing that attracted your attention when you first saw it? Your photo must include that view, aspect, or feeling. Visualize the subject in comparison with its background. Do you want to work the background into the photo, eliminate it all together, or modify it? Then spend some time with your composition. Some outdoor photographers will spend an hour or longer with one shot. You don't have to spend that long with each shot, but some shots really deserve more than a three or four second setup. If you had Kevin Kostner (or Madonna) out there in the woods, you would probably want to take some time to get to know the Subject so you could make your best shot count. If you see a really great Scene, there's no need to "snap-n'run." That one Scene may be the real reason you came out today.

So, take some time to get to know your Subject. Your best view may no longer be "the flower"; it may have become a part of the flower - petals, leaves, and general shape. In this case, the rest of the flower is now playing the role of supporting elements. Note the textures and tones that are (or could be) part of the photo. Study the color scheme from all angles. Make sure they don't distract from the subject. Try to balance the frame with compatible colors, and always keep an eye open for a small amount of sharply contrasting color. It could be that you might have little bits of colored props with you that could be tossed into the frame for that purpose. **Poker chips**, perhaps, one each of blue, red, yellow, and green, or a **bandanna** (red or blue) could do this trick as well. But if you do this, be sure to *blur the prop* so that it is unrecognizable in the photo, and - oh yes - you might want to be sparse with this. You might even decide to carry some costume jewelry (the stuff six-year olds like) with you and put one in each photo (almost hiding it, maybe), to not only add certain colors, but also to establish your very own special mark in each of your photos. Of course, the props will be put back in your photo bag after the shots are finished.

Don't stop with flowers. Many things can be grist for your photo mill! **Rocks**, **spider webs, insects** (butterflies, especially), snow and frost formations (try them up close, especially if you have a macro wide-angle lens). Don't forget tree trunks, particularly dead ones or Birches, and others that have striking textures. A **small spray bottle** can be used to put a fine mist on certain objects such as flowers, leaves, buds, and spider webs. I often carry a small spray nozzle in my vest, and can spray a small amount of water right out of my drinking flask.

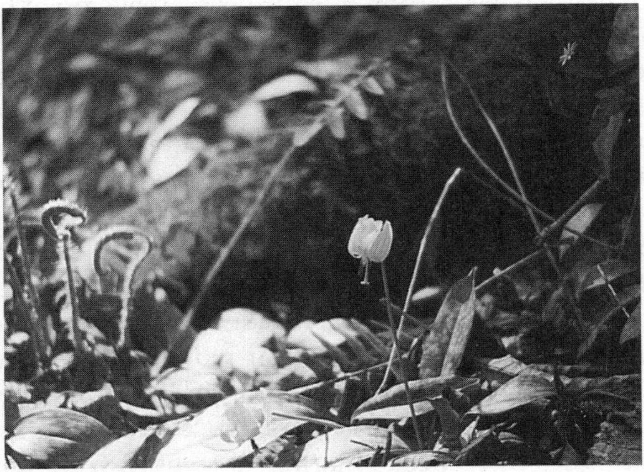

Figure 7.3. Trout Lily.
(*Erythronium americanum*)
Note the glare on the leaves. I had to shoot this on a dark windy day from twenty feet away. So I removed the polarizer filter and still made an eight -second exposure. Note that the mottled leaves of the lily are discern-able. The Subject lily is positioned against the dark log, for visibility, but the other lily is lost in leaf glare.

Chapter Eight

The Camera

The word "Camera" comes from the Latin "camara" and means "vault", or "chamber". The camera chamber is sealed so no rays of light can stray into it. One end of the chamber contains unexposed film that is stretched from one side to the other with a light-sensitive emulsion facing the other end. Just in front of the film is the shutter which can be opened and closed by the photographer. The other end of the camera chamber has a combination of lenses which admit and bend light rays so that a focused image can be presented to the film when the shutter is opened. Between the two is an Aperture Ring which determines how much light will be admitted to the film in a given period of time, and also controls the depth of focus. When the shutter is open, light can enter into the chamber and fall on the light-sensitive emulsion on the film. This process is regulated by the photographer who determines 1) how wide the aperture will be opened and 2) how long the shutter will be left opened. These two decisions underlay much of the science of photography.

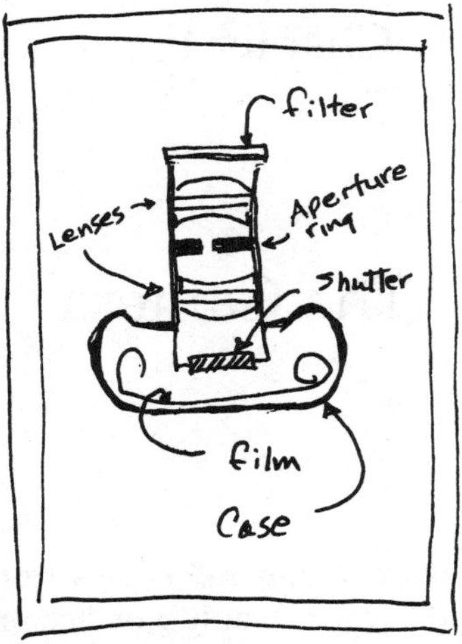

Fig. 8.1
Basic Camera Parts

First, I want to say a word to the most basic of beginning photographers, those who are really beginning beginners: You have the capability to make great photographs, and that capability is actually enhanced by the fact that you don't have a lot of "unlearning" to do.

Let's look at some of the camera controls.

Basically, we will make our photos by adjust the Aperture Opening and the Shutter Speed.

The shutter speed, or the time that the shutter is open, can usually be regulated from several seconds to about 1/1000th of a second. Some cameras have speeds that range from 30 seconds to 1/8000th of a second.

The size of the aperture, can vary from the size of a pinhole (almost) to the entire side of the camera chamber (almost). Obviously, the difference in the amount of light admitted to the chamber would vary greatly depending on whether the opening is 1 millimeter (mm) across or 100mm across.

It can easily be seen that during very dim periods of light, such as occur before sunrise, one would probably open the aperture very wide, and leave the shutter open for a long time. Conversely, on a bright day after a snowfall, one might have the aperture opened to a very small diameter, and leave the shutter open for a very short time. During "average" conditions the aperture can be opened to an "average" diameter and the shutter for an "average" time, or it could be opened wide for a short time, or barely opened for a long period of time.

What factors would a photographer weigh in making this Aperture Size verses Shutter Speed decision? Many photographers first consider the shutter speed requirement. If the picture to be made is that of a wildflower, and there is a very strong wind blowing and the flower is very actively in motion, then the shutter speed will have to take priority. The photographer will have to use a high shutter speed, and then open the aperture wide enough to let more light in during the short time the shutter is open. If the shutter speed does not take priority, then the aperture can be given priority

Let's take another look at the shutter speeds for a moment. Notice how the different speeds have been built into your camera. You don't choose your shutter speed so much as you choose from among shutter speed options that are built into your camera. Also notice how all of these speeds are either twice as fast as the one next to it, or twice as slow as the one next to it, depending on which way you are looking. So you can double the amount of light that comes into your camera chamber by moving to the next slower shutter speed. When you double the amount of light like this, it is sometimes said that you have increased, or added, the amount of light by "One EV", or "One Exposure Value". If you move to the next faster shutter speed, you would cut the amount of light admitted into the camera chamber by half, and you would have decreased, or taken away, the amount of light admitted into the camera by one EV. Most cameras provide settings of 1 second, 1/2 second, then 1/4 second (note, again, the doubling, or halving, of the light factor), the next setting will probably be 1/8 second, (probably shown on your camera as just "8"), then 16 (1/16 second), 32, 64, 125, 250, 500, 1000, 2000, and maybe others. If you have a "B" setting, the "B" means "Brief" or "Bulb", and the shutter will remain open as long as you hold down the shutter release button. Many older camera have a "T" setting. The "T" means "Time", and the shutter will open when you press and release the shutter release button, and it will stay open until the next time you press and release the button.

So, if we have a wildflower that is blowing in the wind, we would probably want to use a fast shutter speed to "freeze" it so we can get a picture of the flower in focus. If the available light is very low, then we will want to use a slower shutter speed. Another reason many outdoor photographers change the shutter speed often occurs when photographing flowing water. Then it is possible to use a fast shutter speed, to "freeze" the flow of the water, or use a slow shutter speed to let the water look more like a ribbon, or to use a mid-range shutter speed so the water looks more natural to the eye, although not necessarily a better photo.

Why would we want to let the size of the aperture take precedent in making the photo? The main reason for doing this is to give the photographer control of the depth of field in the photo. As we mentioned in chapter four, even when a Subject is properly focused, there will often be an area between the photographer and the Subject that will also be in focus, and often an area behind the Subject that will be in focus. We often speak of a "plane of focus" as if the area of focus were very narrow. Usually, though, it is more like a "zone of focus" that extends in front of and behind the subject. The depth of this zone of focus is controlled by the width of the aperture. The more wide open the aperture is, the more shallow is the zone of focus, the narrower the opening of the aperture is, the deeper is the zone of focus.

Suppose you see a deer in the forest. Deer tend to be fairly well camouflaged, and a photo with everything in focus will probably tend to "hide" the deer. You would have to point the deer out to everyone who looked at the picture. But if you could adjust your depth of focus just right, and get only the deer in focus, and blur everything else in front of and behind the deer, then the deer would stand out in the photo just like the old sore thumb. Figure 8.2 shows a cat caught in the act of stalking a bird. Take a good look, the shrubbery in front of the cat is blurred and the woods behind the cat are blurred, but the cat is in pinpoint focus.Sometimes telephone lines, fences,

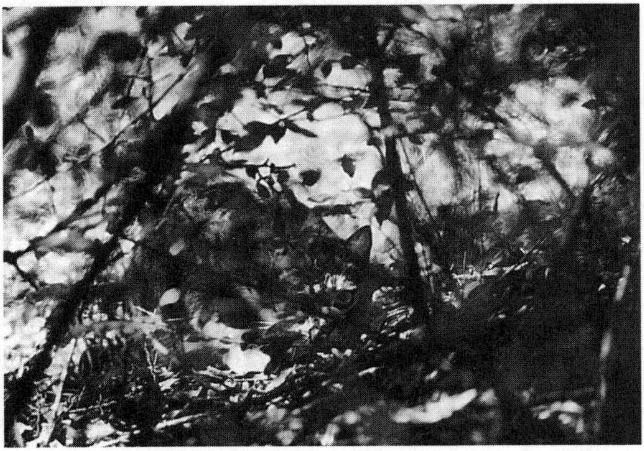

Figure 8.2. Cat caught in the act of stalking. Only the cat is in sharp focus.

even houses and roads can be thrown far enough out of focus as to be rendered totally unnoticeable in the final photo. The wildflower we talked about earlier would be beautiful photographed with a very narrow depth of focus, so that only the flower was in focus. Everything else, the leaves and rocks and grass in the foreground could be blurred, and the rocks and trees in the background could be blurred into a very pleasing backdrop somewhat like the backdrops that some portrait photographers use when they make photos of people in their studios. Some cameras have a "depth of field preview button", and when you press that button you can see what will be in focus and what will be out of focus. Many cameras have a depth of field scale that is arranged symmetrically around the distance index. If your camera has such a depth of field scale, you will notice two figures for each aperture opening option, on either side of a center line. The distances shown on the distance index that are opposite each of the aperture setting markers that have been set into the camera indicates the depth of focus.

The depth of focus is controlled by the size of the opening of the aperture, but the distance from the lens to the Subject also plays a crucial role. The closer to the Subject the photographer is, the more likely the depth of focus will be measured in inches instead of feet. So, you could stand in a field with wildflowers at your feet, and by using a very small aperture opening, make your depth of focus so long that the flowers at your feet would be in focus and so would the mountains that are out on the horizon. Or, if you wished to do so, you could open your aperture so wide that only the wild flower would be in focus and the mountains would be blurred, or the mountains could be in focus and the flowers blurred. (Of course as you went to a smaller sized aperture opening, which would admit less light into the camera, you would slow your shutter speed, and as you went to the wider aperture opening which would admit more light into the camera, you would have to increase your shutter speed.)

The depth of field can also be modified by changing the focal length of the lens. The focal length of the lens is the distance from the outermost piece of glass in the lens to the film plane. 50mm is considered to be "normal" because that is the approximate distance from corner to corner of the negative frame. Any lens shorter than 50mm is considered to be a "wide-angle" lens, and any lens longer than 50mm is said to be tele-photo. A "zoom" lens is a lens whose focal length can be changed while the photographer is looking through it. As the focal length increases, the depth of field will decrease.

Aperture opening sizes can be changed by the photographer, and like the shutter speed, they are normally selected from sizes already built into your camera. Aperture sizes are also arranged in sizes that result in either the doubling or halving of the diameter with each adjustment. The size of the opening is stated relative to the length of the lens that is on the camera. If the opening is 1/2 the size of the length of the lens it will be stated as f/2. If it is 1/4 the length of the lens, it will be stated as f/4. So you can see that the larger the f/number, the smaller will be the size of the aperture opening. F/22 is smaller than f/4, in the same manner in which a hole that is 1/22nd of an inch is smaller than one that is 1/4th of an inch. Since the aperture opening is roundish, the sizes do not increase in a 1, 2, 4, 8, 16 progression; instead, 1.4 is half the size of 1, and 1.8 is half the size of 1.4, and then the sizes run on a scale of 1 and 1.4, as follows: 1, 1.4, 2, 2.8, 4, 5.6, 8,

11, 16, 22, 32, 45. Each of these f/numbers admits 1/2 the amount of light into the chamber than the preceding one admitted.

Now, what about film speed? The film speed depends, let us say, on the size of crystals in the film emulsion. The greater the size of the crystals, the greater the "speed" of the film, that is, the greater the ability of the film to gather enough light to register an image in a given amount of time. Film "speed" is represented by an **ISO** (International Standards Organization) Number. You may see references to an ASA (American Standards Association) Number. That has been replaced by ISO numbers and ISO is identical to ASA, that is ASA 100 = ISO 100. All ISO "speeds" or ratings are relative to each other, and the "speed" of the film doubles as the ISO number doubles. Film with an ISO number of 400 is twice as "fast" as film with an ISO number of 200, which, in turn, is twice as "fast" as film which is rated with an ISO number of 100. The EV rating applies here too, because if you change film speed from ISO 100 to 200, your EV has also increased by one.

There is a corresponding disadvantage to increased "speed" of film, and that disadvantage is that the "**graininess**" of the final picture will increase as the film "speed" increases. Film with an ISO rating of 40 will usually produce a picture with images having very sharp detail and vivid color. Film with an ISO rating of 3200 often produce a picture with images having much less vivid detail and some color "shift" or variance from the actual color. The 3200 ISO film, of course, will permit the photographer to make hand-held pictures by candlelight, while 40 ISO film often requires the use of a tripod even under bright daylight conditions. The "graininess" of the higher ISO film will probably not be a significant factor as long as the ISO rating remains at 400 or below <u>and</u> size of the final print is not greater than 16" X 20". However, the very best photographs that can be made for reprinting in magazines such as National Geographic, will almost always be made from transparencies which had an ISO number of about 100 or less.

You will stock your gear bag with film of ISO 400 rating or higher if you are going to Joyce Kilmer, or some dark forest on a cloudy day, but with ISO 100 or less if you are going to be trekking the higher peaks after a snowfall on a bright day. It's usually good to hedge this bet by taking one or two rolls of film on the other end of the spectrum of film speed; the best photo you could make could well be one you didn't expect to see.

If you notice a "DIN" number on the film, that is a European designation (Deutsche Industrie Norm) and its film speed doubles with each DIN increase of 3: DIN 21 = ISO 100, DIN 24 = ISO 200, DIN 27 = ISO 400.

Remember to protect your lenses. Lens covers often don't seem to work well because they are often hard to find, get dropped, etc. Many photographers protect their expensive lenses with an inexpensive <u>filter</u>, usually a "**Skylight**" or "**UV" (for ultraviolet) filter**. These filters can be cleaned by you, and your lens probably shouldn't be; the filters can take fingerprints and be cleaned, can be scratched and later replaced. There are even tales of these filters being broken, and the lens surviving.

Also remember there are two uncovered lenses, the front lens, and the rear lens. They are both delicate and expensive. At least, the rear lens is covered whether it is in a bag or on the camera, but the front lens is still vulnerable when it is on the camera unless it has a filter on it. The glass part of the lenses are extremely precise elements. In order to transmit light properly, most of them have been coated with a precision coating. That coating must not be scratched or cleaned off, either. Three of the worst enemies of lenses and their coating, are dust, fingerprints and cleaning fluids. One would never touch the glass part of a lens, because fingerprints carry (and often deposit on the lens) dirt, oil and even acid. Cleaning the lenses is a precise job requiring specific techniques and equipment and is one that you would not want to do unless you have received direct observation instruction from a qualified professional. Glass cleaners, detergents, and most other cleaners are not to be used either.

My camera often gets switched by limbs and leaves while hiking in tight places, especially late on a long day. I did scratch some coating off an expensive wide-angle zoom lens late in the day coming down off of Chunky Gal Trail. And yes, I do understand that many professional photographers and photojournalists do not use those protective filters over their lenses, because they feel that they reduce the amount of light reaching the film. Some points one might consider when determining whether or not to use those protective filters: 1) the professionals may have better insurance, 2) their lenses may be underwritten by a company they work for, 3) if they need to replace lenses, it probably will be handled as a business expense, 4) they may have better habits as far as handling, switching and storing lenses than they did when they were just starting their work, and 5) they probably have the necessary equipment and experience to clean their lenses from time to time. So make your decision as appropriate for you. Why don't the professionals like those filters in front of their lenses? They say the lenses take some of the light away by distortion, reflection, refraction, and help pick up lens flare. Also, they say, since the filters are out in front of the camera, they scratch very easily. My advice is to get a filter, put it on and use it. As your photography skills develop, then come back and revisit this idea. One last word: the last time I fell while hiking was out of Deep Gap, near Standing Indian Mountain, on a muddy hillside. I fell on the camera (which hurts!), and the thing was covered with mud. I wiped it off with my bandanna, and then I simply took off the UV filter, squirted water from my flask over it, dried it off and put it back on the camera. Without the filter, the objective lens of my $400 zoom lens would have absorbed all that gritty mud.

What's the most neglected document in the world today? Probably the book of instructions that comes with most cameras. They serve some purpose at first, but then we tend to figure it out as we go. If you still have that book, dig it out and spend some time with it. I will guarantee that you will learn a number of things, and at least one of those will probably turn out to be very useful. Spend some time, go over the book with camera in hand and make a list of what you found out that surprised you.

Also, make some **dry runs**. Next time your camera is out of film, make some snaps, changing those settings that you use often when making pictures; then try some new settings. Practice using the capabilities your camera has that you are not familiar with. Work at it until you find out something you didn't know. If you have a Single Lens Reflex, and you change lenses, make some dry runs doing this. These practices are important; think of the recruit learning to take his rifle apart and reassemble it while blindfolded, and think how that capability may save his life on a distant battlefield in the smoke and mud of combat, or of the professional football team walking slowly through a very complicated play that they will later execute with lightning speed in a critical moment in the big game.

Chapter Nine

Equipment and Accessories

The only filters I use are ultraviolet (UV) or Skylight for lens protection, and a polarizing filter for darkening the sky and removing glare from reflections. I do not have a graduated neutral density filter, but intend to get one to use on overcast days when I have to include some sky, or when photographing water that has a strong sky reflection. I may eventually get a "warming" or "cooling" filter.

What about tripods? There really isn't a good way to make good outdoor photographs without one. But you need a good tripod; a cheap one is worse than none at all. I use a Bogen 3021. What I like about it is: 1) it is steady; 2) it's legs are open, with no braces between them; 3) it has controls placed so that they can be operated by the left hand leaving the right hand free for the camera controls; 4) the legs can be easily adjusted to compensate for uneven ground; 5) it can be set up from about 6.5 feet above the ground, down to about 6 inches high; 6) the adjustments for leg height are really adjustable. 7) It is indestructible. I use a Bogen 3055 Super Ball head to connect the camera to the tripod. It becomes a part of the camera base and snaps on and off of the tripod quickly. I like it because: 1) it grips the camera extraordinarily well; 2) it goes vertical in three slots; 3) it is strong enough to carry the camera attached to the tripod. What about weight? The tripod and head that I use weigh 14 pounds. I will carry them on a six hour hike and use them to make three or four photos sometimes. Is it worth that? If you want to get great photos, you will probably want to use slide film rated at ISO 40 to 100; that means if you don't take the tripod, you don't take the camera. Sometimes it is the only difference between an outstanding shot and a snapshot.

Amazingly, aluminum tripod legs transfer heat about as effectively as an ice cube does. When the outside temperature gets below about 60°, the tripod legs get uncomfortably cold. I recommend buying pipe insulator to place around the tripod legs. The stuff is cheap, less than two dollars for about six feet. It can be cut to size, and you really don't need to cover the entire leg system of the tripod, I find that one piece about five inches long, placed on one leg is usually sufficient.

Clothing? Blue jeans are the most practical pants I have found, sometimes I will use other color jeans if I plan to stop off and sell some books or photos. Cotton tee shirts and long sleeved cotton shirts are good for all seasons. I always carry a hooded nylon windbreaker and hooded cotton sweatshirt if I am going above 5,000 feet, even in the summer, although I won't carry the sweatshirt if hiking. In the winter, I go prepared to hike back out in heavy snow or freezing rain, and strong winds. Head gear consists of a cap if hiking in the woods or hiking hat or tennis hat if I plan to spend a lot of time in the sun; I always carry a knit cap in cold weather. Hats and caps are also great for keeping stray sunbeams out of the lens of your camera. When I shoot from a tripod, I set my camera on self-timer mode for three to five seconds before it fires the shot so that I don't shake the camera when pressing the shutter - that also gives me time to use cap or hat to shade the lens opening from sun glare if that seems necessary.

Footwear must be hiking boots if on hiking trails in the Blue Ridge mountains. They can save sprained or broken ankles and help you get up and down steep slopes; they also dry out quicker than shoes. I won't go on a hiking trail without wearing hiking boots. Back at the truck, I often have sandals, trail shorts, and polo shirt. Nice to change into after a long hike, and also OK for shooting from parking areas.

I usually wear a vest when shooting because it carries filters, unexposed film, exposed film, brush, small spray nozzle, permanent marking pen, sun reflectors, bandanna, lens cloth, compass and tripod wrench. A small fanny pack which hangs in front carries another lens for my camera. If I am hiking I also wear a larger fanny pack that hangs in the rear which carries lunch, snake bite kit, first aid kit, lighter, piece of candle, flashlight, very small needle nosed Vise Grip, a large Swiss Army knife, folded duct tape and gaffer tape and a half gallon of water. I can tie onto the bottom of the fanny pack a poncho, sweat shirt and shelter cloth if I wish to. If I don't carry my sketch book hiking, I do have a small spiral notebook (3 x 5 inches) that can take notes for later transfer. Often I carry a tape recorder and a second or third camera (sometimes point-and-shoot). And oh yes, usually a tripod. The truck always has at least one gallon of drinking water in it.

In the truck I also keep a small piece of plastic tarp, about 2 x 4 feet. This is great for those low-level shots, usually of wildflowers, where you have to get down on your knees or even lay down, and it's even better if the ground is wet.

Miscellanea includes a film leader retriever. It is occasionally very valuable, but also takes a good bit of practice and patience to make it work. A small flashlight is sometimes important, and usually unnecessary. Filter wrenches are great for getting stuck filters off, although now I use small pieces (about 4" x 5") of that woven rubber material that is used under "throw" rugs (to keep them from "throwing" people). My Nikon 8008 is dead if it has no batteries so I always carry at least eight spares. (I carry them in the truck, not on my person.) The camera uses four AA batteries and so does the flash. I also want to allow for new batteries that don't work, and if necessary, I can switch them out of the flash. In my camera bag, I carry a large plastic garbage bag that I can put the whole thing into in case of a hard rain, and I carry a smaller trash bag, that the camera will fit into, in a small film tube on the camera strap. I also like to have a cotton glove for handling film and I carry one wound up and tucked into an old clear plastic film canister to keep it clean. I have a large brush in my camera bag to go with the one on my vest. I use that to brush off the canister lip before loading the film into the camera, and often to clean off the filters before shooting.

I carry the camera bag in the vehicle only, and seldom take it out of there. When hiking, I usually carry the camera under my left arm, with the neck strap passing over my head, and resting on my right shoulder. I realize that many photographers carry their camera under one arm and with the strap resting on that same shoulder, but that is not safe while hiking in the forest. I gave that up after my second drop. My experience shows that each drop of the camera costs an average of about $150 in repairs. Often I will carry the camera on the tripod, with the tripod legs extended and rest it on my shoulder. If you want to be able to make quick shots of surprise targets you encounter while hiking, I would recommend you carry a smaller camera available in your vest or other pocket. Your main camera, film, tripod, etc. is really dedicated to well thought-out shots.

I usually do not carry a flash while hiking. It remains at the truck. However, if the mission is to get certain rare wildflowers, and the woods are dark, the sky is overcast, and the wind is blowing, I will carry the flash.

A record of places and times is an invaluable resource tool for an outdoor photographer. I call mine a "sketch book" because I sometimes do make sketches in it, but usually it is a roughly written log of my journeys, especially by vehicle. I number each right hand page and then, beginning at the last page put in an index of sorts. I will write an "A" at the top of the page, skip several lines and put a "B", then follow with a "C" and a "D" near the bottom. Then next page will get the next four letters, and so on. That takes up the last three or four pages of the sketch book. Then I will make entries as appropriate by day, beginning from the front. As the book fills up, I may make a journey across, say, Patterson Gap Road on July 4, 2001. I will then enter, July 4, 2001 (or 010704), write "Patterson Gap Road" next to it or below it, then get a departure fix from some permanent object, and enter items of interest as the journey progresses. Let's say this entry is made on page 36. When I am through with the trip, I will turn to the index, and under "P", write "Patterson Gap Road 36. Now, I can review this trip when I need to, whether it is next week or three years from now. Also, I will enter items of interest that I saw while on the trip. If I saw Indian Paint Brush, then I will turn to the index under "I" and mark that the Indian Paint Brush is on page 36. Also, trilliums, oswego tea, will go under "T" and "O". Eventually, on a cold April morning, I can turn to "D" in each book and look up "Dutchmans'-breeches" and find a number of references to where I can go to photograph them. This is not a complete diary; it is a very rough log with barely enough information to make sense. <u>But</u>, when I find a great view or scene, then the information becomes much more precise and meaningful. I also use this sketch book, or others, when on trips to the beach, or Arizona, Florida, California, Europe, Asia, etc. This way, I always have places to find my way back to, and also there are comments about places I didn't get to, but will, next time.

Many years ago, when I began making outdoor photographs, I began by just driving and hiking, more or less aimlessly. Now when I go out, I can go dancing.

Chapter Ten

The Dancing Trail

One of the finest parts of a good photographic course is the opportunity to work outdoors as a class, where new students can watch their instructor and other photographers work. That is obviously not possible to do through the medium of writing. So in this chapter I will discuss some of the processes that I use when photographing.

My own personal approaches toward making outdoor photographs take advantage of many different methods. Often it seems that some of the best photos I get are those I shoot off my deck, or on the pathways that wind through the woods around our house. But I do a lot of hiking, too, and a lot of shooting from various highways, such as those that run up to Wayah Bald, Standing Indian Mountain Campground area, Albert Mountain, the Cullasaja Gorge, the Cherohala Skyway, the Blue Ridge Parkway and many other of the great roadways in and around Macon County, North Carolina. Sometimes, I react to a scene, grabbing my camera and shooting at a sunset or a bird.

Most often, however, I will work from a plan. If I will be shooting from the Blue Ridge Parkway, I will pick several days out of the month for possible trips up there. As the week for the excursion approaches, I will monitor the weather and make more precise plans and determine places I would like to be in hourly increments. If I plan to be in an area from morning to sunset, I will plan certain photos for different hours of the day. It is easy to determine the direction and altitude of the sun (See Appendix A), and I will plan various vistas to take advantage of sidelighting, frontal and back lighting. During the 10:00 a.m. to 2:00 p.m. period of high sun, I will plan to eat, hike to locations for flower shots and other detail photos which can be made under the shade of the forest, or I may write or do watercolors, but usually I do not make landscape photographs during this period. I *will* usually consider making some shots on downward sloping northern or northwestern or northeastern mountain sides if shadows are lengthened sufficiently by the gradient, and often plan to eat lunch at such locations. I may also reposition myself, my vehicle and equipment, to prepare for photos to come after the sun has changed its position. Later in the afternoon, I will try to be in places to take advantage of the sun angles as they become more useable, and then work my way back out of the area or to a particular vantage point as sunset approaches.

The planning includes a review of my slides to see what I feel is lacking. Actually, I keep a "Want List" which I update constantly. I may need a certain late summer wildflower like a Bee Balm or Turk's Cap Lily, or I may want to replace a shot of Lone Bald that doesn't have any real depth to it. The "Want List" may have as many as 100 photos that I want to take. I will choose those that are appropriate to the time of year for this trip, I will schedule the time of day for some of them, knowing where the sunlines will be at those hours to get sidelighting, backlighting, or 4545R, and try to take advantage of a logical progression of driving. Other days may be dedicated to a really elusive landscape shot, and I may go prepared to spend several hours in one spot all set up and ready to make that one shot. Other times I may just run out on the spur of the moment for a trip because the day is too good to *not* go shooting! Even then I will still have my "Want List", my topographical maps, my "sketch" book, and all the needs necessary to subsist for a few hours out on the range.

When I approach a shot, I will first consider the View, that portion of the universe that is visible at that time. I usually employ the Interpretive Compositional elements first. What impressions, non-physical qualities, feelings, characteristics, emotions or moods are evoked by the Objects, Scenes or

Views that I sense? This may take a little time, and may lead me to other locations where various scenes of that view may be observed.

I may know that I am looking at a wonderful View, but it may take a while for me to clear my mind enough to sense what elements are coming through. As I begin to feel that I know what seems to be calling to me, then I will begin bringing in some Expressive Compositional options; these two aspects seem to work together, like two dancers dancing, rather than in any linear, logically sequential fashion. What seems to be calling to me; what feelings do I experience? How do I want to present the feelings I have experienced? Do I want to try to do this as great symbols? How do I want to tell the story? Are there critical moments available or imminent - such as sunset, or maybe cloud shadows drifting across certain ridgelines? Are there several stories available? What do I wish was there that I haven't noticed yet? Then I will begin to feed in some of the Technical Composition part. I will consider film, tone, viewpoint, color. What is the overall colorcast of the part of nature I want in the picture? Is it likely that the colorcast might change in the near future? How can I balance a certain color with a harmonious or contrasting one? Should I try monochromatic, harmonic, balance or contrast color schemes? What about contrast? Is it a problem? What is my EV spread from dark to light? Will I need to adjust my exposure reading? How can I minimize (or intensify) that area that is going to be too dark? What about glare, and how should I handle it? How does all of this modify the Interpretive and Expressive composition? Finally, I will review the Design Composition possibilities. Do I want to use Rule of Thirds? How about Unsymmetrical Division? Light and dark, repetitions, balance, lines and curves - do I want to use any of them, just one of them, or several of them together? What seems the best way to attract the viewers' eye and lead into the photo and hold it there? How can I communicate what I feel?

How long does all this take? Sometimes, only several minutes. Sometimes several hours. I do not seek a structured format because I feel that tends to subdue and disconnect artistic connections. Even if I do not get a single photograph, if I get good feelings and attunement, the trip is a success! I can always come back, and photographs are easier when you know what is really there. Often, I return to certain Sites again and again over years before I get a picture I am satisfied with (for a while!), anyway. Then someone will ask how did I make that picture?

Many times I will size up a Site, set up the camera and tripod and not make even one picture. Sometimes I will set up and make a photo in a few minutes, and then wait for an hour or so before I make the next one, or will leave, (with the camera!) and come back later. Before I leave a Site, I will write in my "sketch" book impressions I have received, and suggestions for revisits later, or in other seasons, or different times of the day.

When I approach a brand new shoot, a place to which I have never been, I will begin by establishing a dossier of information about it. (I try to keep a catalog of such places on hand.) Any writing by other authors, or photographs, would go into the dossier, also road maps, so I know how to get there and back and have approximate time data for a schedule. Topographic maps will be added to the dossier and studied to see if they have useable shooting information available. As the date becomes roughly scheduled, I will add sun angles and moonrise/set times to the dossier, and consider the aspects of the seasons involved: it may be summer, yes, but is it early or late summer? This may seem a trivial point, but in the mountains, it is a big deal! Or is it in a subsidiary season as well, such as the Dog Days, or Blackberry Winter, or maybe Indian Summer? Is it approaching a Cross Quarter day such as mid-summer? What wild flowers can I expect to see? What historical data is available? How much of it is factual? What questions do they raise? I try to consider current, recent, civil war, settler, Indian, ancient histories. What is different about this place than other places? I will try to pick out sites from the map and make some rough shot schedules. Sometimes when I get to a scene, and talk to local residents, I find that I know more about the place than they do - and I have never been there before! But then, they will have information I don't, and that will also find it's way into the dossier.

When I arrive on Scene, I will record locations in my "sketch" book. As I enter the area, I will find some permanent and easy to find marker such as a road intersection, old building, etc., and use that as a starting point, sort of a "departure fix". Graveyards are excellent for this, because you know they will be there the next time you come back.

From there I will record distances or times as I enter into the area, and will update and restart that as I progress. So, if I find a great view from a gravel pull-off, I will know that it is 7.3 miles from the intersection of Grimm Gap Road and Blue Cow Lane. I can find it again. Often I will hike out from these areas and keep a record of those hikes and finds. Next time I come to this place I will have starting points, and a better schedule. I will do some sketching and visualize how a view might look in winter, autumn or spring, or at sunrise, sunset, good weather, bad weather, etc. I will be prepared to make great slide shots on that first trip, but will probably make most of my shots on the first trip using color print ISO 400 film, and do a lot of wide-angle work. Some of these will be added to the dossier, and will form the basis for planning future shots. Some of them will be good enough to put on note cards, or even enlarge into 8 x 12 prints. Some will find their way into the computer for manipulation and processing. Some may be used for watercolor sketches. Others will just be seeds for future trips. Some of them may eventually "turn into" great slide shots that will be made on a later trip.

When the shoot is over, I put the cameras back to fully automatic mode, and place them in their camera bag in the truck. Now if I encounter a great Scene, while driving, I can make my first shot without having to check settings. When I get to another shoot, I will put them back into manual mode, and resume The Dance.

When hiking, I will review, if possible, the trail before the hike. If I have been there before, I will review my past "log", which may or may not have been transcribed and written up as a trail guide. I usually log my hikes on a microcassette tape recorder, by making a comment whenever I see a good View, Site, Subject, etc., and try to make a comment at least every ten minutes. Later, I will transcribe that onto a legal pad, and from there, it finds its way into the computer. If it is a new hike, I will scrutinize the trail on a topographic map under a magnifying glass a day or two before the trip. I will spend an hour or two on this and make out a rough "flight plan", estimating the time to cover various distances (my thumbwidth is about ten minutes hiking time on a 1:24,000 topo map) and try to visualize what might be available in various places. If the trail turns around a ridge with a steep fall off to one side and a high ridge to the other, I have an idea of what it might look like. If it is a low spot with a creek crossing it, I have another idea of what I might find there. Now, how about the sun angle? What time of the year? Should there be crowfoot, trillium, umbrella plant, fire pink, Indian paint brush, New Jersey tea, bee balm, Turk's cap lily, etc., at these places? What about the trees, the south side of a ridge line should have pines and oaks (what kind of birds are likely to be there?). Hardwood cove areas will have river birch, moosewood, maples, etc., (what kind of birds might I expect to find there?) How about rock formations, and boulder fields? So when I hike, I am constantly finding what I expected to find, and am constantly surprised at what is not there or what is *really* there!

On a muggy summer day, I may see a View

that is not very good, and don't take any pictures, but I know it may be full of fantastic Scenes on a brilliant autumn day. I will make careful note of that in my old sketch book, complete with directions and instructions about how to get back. It may be a few months or even a year or two before I do get back, but some brilliant autumn day you might see me there, perched with my tripod on the far end of a ridge, high above a great blue valley now gilded with red and gold, peering through my viewfinder looking at pure glory, as I dance with joy and make great pictures!

Come and join me there!

Apendix A

Sun Times & Azumuths for 45° Elevation

The following figures indicate the aproximate **Eastern Standard Time** at which the sun will pass through the 45° elevation on the first day of the months in which it rises above that elevation.

Example: on April 1, the sun will rise through 45° at 11:05 a.m., and descend below 45° later at 2:10 p.m. At 11:05 a.m., the sun will be located at an azimuth of 158° from north, and at 2:10 p.m., it will be at an azimuth of 202° from north. Shadows will be cast 180° from the azimuth of the sun. At 2:10 p.m., on April 1, the shadow of a tree, or mountain peak, will fall toward 022°. (202° minus 180°, or 022°.)

Date	A.M.	Azimuth	P.M.	Azimuth
Mar 1	12:30	176	1:05	187
Apr 1	11:05	158	2:10	202
May 1	10:05	144	3:00	220
Jun 1	9:33	130	3:30	230
Jul 1	9:35	129	3:35	231
Aug 1	10:00	136	3:18	224
Sep 1	10:40	153	2:30	215
Oct 1	11:40	167	1:06	190

(Add one hour for DST, if and when in use)

These tables are derived for 35.5N 83.5W, a central location for the southern Blue Ridge mountains.

Appendix B

Sun Table

	Sunrise		Sunset		Maximum
Date	Time	Azimuth	Time	Azimuth	Sun Elev
Jan 1	7:42	118	5:33	242	32
Feb 1	7:33	110	6:02	250	38
Mar 1	7:03	98	6:29	261	48
Apr 1	6:20	83	6:55	276	59
May 1	5:43	70	7:19	289	70
Jun 1	5:21	62	7:43	298	77
Jul 1	5:23	60	7:52	299	78
Aug 1	5:43	67	7:36	292	73
Sep 1	6:06	79	7:00	280	63
Oct 1	6:29	93	6:17	266	52
Nov 1	6:55	107	5:39	252	40
Dec 1	7:24	116	5:22	243	33

(Add one hour for DST, if and when in use.)

These tables present **Eastern Standard Time** and azimuth of sunrise and sunset for the first day of each month, and the maximum elevation reached by the sun on that day. They are approximate figures for the southern Blue Ridge Mountains (derived for 35.5°N, 83.5°W). Although the times, azimuths and elevations are accurate, they are not precise. If precise figures are *critical* for your work, there are many excellent astronomical computer compact discs that will provide this data. Earliest sunset occurs Dec 4, latest sunrise Jan 7; earliest sunrise June 14, latest sunset June 29.

Appendix C

Note concerning the effect of the sun when it is higher than 45° above the horizon:[1]

This effect depends on not only the time of day, but also, the season of the year, and the location of the photographer or subject. At north latitude of 35.5°, on June 21, the sun will reach 45° altitude at 9:29 a.m. en route to a peak of 79°. It will fall below 45° again, 6 hours and 13 minutes later at 3:42 p.m. On September 1, the elevation of 45° will be reached at 10:40, and after reaching a maximum elevation of 63°, it will fall below 45° again just 3 hours and 50 minutes later at 2:30 p.m. On October 1, the sun will reach a maximum elevation of only 52°, and remain above 45° only from 11:40 a.m. until 1:06 p.m. On October 17, 45° is the maximum elevation reached by the sun that day, and it will not reach that elevation again until February 22. On December 21, the maximum elevation achieved by the sun is only 31°.

So, perhaps the rule of thumb which states that lighting is often not good for photographs between 10 and 2, could be modified to state that this is true during months which do not fall between 10 and 2 ("10", now representing not 10 o'clock, but the tenth month, October; and "2" representing not 2 o'clock, but February.) So: **"Don't shoot between 10 and 2, except between 10 and 2."**

Also, keep in mind that while 45° is considered by some to be the optimum elevation of a primary light, it is not a limit of operations. 46° is OK, so is 48, 50 and even above, just as would be 40° or 35°. It is just that once you pass 45°, (either direction) you are moving into an area of more challenging photography; although the lower elevations generally provide more dramatic photos, and the higher elevations tend to increase contrast and flatten out perspective. Also, on an overcast day, a high sun may provide great photos of flowers and other detail objects (and you will remember to keep that overcast sky out of the photo frame).

How can you measure the elevation of the sun relative to 45° above the horizon? Compare the horizontal length of the shadow of any object that has a known vertical height. The object could be the length of your walking staff, or your own height. If you are six feet tall, when the sun is 45° high in the sky, your shadow will be six feet long. If your shadow is longer than you are tall, the sun is below 45°; if your shadow is shorter than you are tall, then the sun is higher than 45° in the sky. You will probably find your best shooting occurs when your shadow is between 75% of your height, and twice your height.

How about shooting on downward sloping north sides of mountains when the sun is above 45°? This can work, although the brightness may still be a problem.

[1] Data obtained using *Redshift* CD-ROM from Maris.

Appendix D

Calendar

This calendar is only *roughly* approximate (if that!). The elevation in the mountain area varies from about 1,500 to 6,500 feet, and the fall and spring seasons can be up to four weeks early or late!

Jan Snow and ice. Clear skies, great vast vistas. January Thaw.
Feb First green out of the ground. Daffodils. Maples have red flowers,
Mar Very early flowers, Dutchman's-breeches, trout lilies, squirrel corn, larkspur, bloodroot, violets, first leaves, also trilliums, serviceberry trees, dogwoods may bloom.
Apr New Green, all the leaves come out. Spring wildflowers abound: Indian paint brush, buttercup, daisies, bellwort, dogwoods, flame azaleas, Solomon seals.
May The high altitude oaks leaf out, also spring wildflowers, mayapple, Indian paint brush, wild strawberries, blackberries, chestnuts & sourwoods begin leaf out, maples in full leaf, ash flowers. Spring wildflowers.
Jun Haze, still early to mid-spring above 5,000 ft. Purple Coneflowers, fire-pinks bloom, summer wild flowers begin bloom.
Jul Summer wild flowers. Monarda family, Queen Anne's lace, Turks cap lily, summer wild flowers will max out!

Aug First autumnal blushes, dogwoods begin to turn, goldenrod in bloom. Late summer wildflowers
Sep High country autumn. Blue asters in bloom, dogwoods & sourwood turn red; oaks begin slow turn.
Oct The big show! Birches first, bright yellow; then maples. Sourwoods become purple, chestnuts yellow, beeches orange, hickories yellow, poplar trees go yellow
Nov "Winter" with nice temperatures (usually). Birds abound, The great leaf fall, neighbors and mountain ridges appear.
Dec Snows

The flowers and trees mentioned above are only the most token representatives of the 1,300 or so that you may find in these mountains. Spring, for example, can begin in February around Franklin at 2,400 feet, and not really arrive at Richland Balsam 24 miles away, but at 6,080 feet, until the second week in May. I have heard it said, although I cannot provide a reference for the statement, that 1,000 feet in vertical elevation is equal to 300 miles in northward travel as far as climactic change is concerned. If that is true then the difference between Franklin and Richland Balsam is equivalent to almost 1,200 miles. The higher mountains experience similar climactic conditions as one might expect to encounter about the latitude of Edmonton, Alberta, James Bay, or Central Newfoundland.

Appendix E

Long Exposures

Scene	ISO	Aperture	Shutter Speed
Campfire, faces	400	5.6	1/8 to 2
Campfires, flames	400	2.8	1/30
Comets*			
Fog or rain**			
Lightning	any	11	B or T
Moon ***	any	8	1/ISO
Moonlit landscapes	400	1.4	30
Moonlit snowscapes	400	1.4	15
Sky, > SR or < SS	100	16	1/2 to 1/4
Water, flowing			1/60 to 8 or <
TV images			1/30 or longer

* Comets: use film of ISO 800, 1600, at f/1.8 for 80 mm lens or f/4 for 50 mm or shorter. Expose at 15, 30, 45, 60, 75, 90, 105, and 120 sec. If exposure is longer than 2 min., tail may appear to bend.
** Fog or rain. Expose normally, if fog is light, ADD 1/2 to 1 EV, if dark, subtract 1/2 to 1 EV.
** *The moon appears to move too fast to use very long exposure. Even one or two seconds will start to give you a "sausage" instead of a moon.

Note: these settings are only starting points. If you want the photo badly, make several, and bracket them well.

COLOR PHOTOGRAPHS

Cover: Yellowstone Falls at Graveyard Fields, Blue Ridge Parkway, milemarker 418. Fuji Velvia.

Plate I: High country mixture of Fraser Firs and Red Maple. Overcast day with rain. Fuji Velvia.

Plate II: Summer Wildflowers. Blue Ridge Parkway, milemarker 437. Firepink, Mountain Phlox, Fuji Provia.

Plate III: View of Looking Glass. Blue Ridge Parkway, milemarker 422. Fuji Velvia.

Plate IV: Turk's Cap Lily (*Lilium superbum*) and Swallowtail. Fuji Velvia.

Plate V: Enchanted Forest. Appalachian Trail from Wayah Bald to Wayah Crest. Fuji Velvia.

Plate VI: Snow on the Driveway. Stamey Mountain Road, North Carolina. Fuji Velvia.

Plate VII: Cool Water. Nantahala River, at Standing Indian Campground, North Carolina. Fuji Velvia.

Plate VIII: First Point of Aries: First sunset of the spring. Macon County, North Carolina. Fuji Velvia.

Glossary

Aperture. An adjustable opening, the size of which is controlled by the photographer, that determines how much light can be admitted into the camera. Corresponds to the iris or pupil in the human eye. The size of the aperture also controls the depth of focus.

Distractions. Objects seen in the photo, or in the view, that do not support or modify the subject as desired by the photographer.

Elements. Any Object that is used by a photographer in composing a photograph that supports or modifies the subject.

Exposure Value. Often referred to as "EV". Theoretically, the light from one candle, one foot away from a Subject for one second. Used in a more practical sense to indicate the doubling or halving of the amount of light permitted into the chamber. Increasing the light by one EV would mean opening up the aperture by one setting (doubling the opening) or increasing the exposure time to the next setting (selecting a shutter speed twice as long as the previous one).

Filters. Glass or plastic discs that are placed over the lenses to modify some aspect of light that enters into the camera. Polaroid filters are used to darken the sky, and remove glare. Graduated Neutral Density filters are used to reduce the amount of light from a portion of the scene, UV (UltraViolet) Skylight filters are basically used to protect the lens. Warming and cooling filters either add a small amount of yellow or blue to the light.

Focal length. Distance, measured in mm, from outside of lens to film.

4545R. This refers to positioning the Subject so that the main source of light is coming from 45° above its horizon, 45° from its axis between the photographer and the Subject, and that it has some Reflection from the other side.

F/stop. A measurement of the width of the aperture opening expressed as a fraction of the focal length of the lens.

Film Speed. A measure of the quickness in which different films can form an image. Expressed as ISO numbers.

Frame. The contents of a photograph or viewfinder.

Impression. A non-physical quality, characteristic, feeling, emotion or mood evoked by an Object, Scene or View.

ISO. International Standards Organization. Used in reference to film as a measure of the quickness of image formation. ISO 400 is twice as fast as ISO 200, which is twice as fast as ISO 100.

Location. A general place with access to Views. Often a parking place from which Sites can be reached.

Millimeter: Unit of measurement using metric system, about the width of a straight pin.

Monochromatic. A picture that basically uses one color such as light blue, medium blue and dark blue

Object. Anything which is perceived by the senses of the photographer and can be used as a subject for a photograph or to modify or support a subject either by including in or excluding from the frame.

Scene. A portion of a View that may contain Objects, Subjects or Elements.

Site. A specific place or position, in a Location from which Scenes can be viewed, photographic equipment can be set up, and photographs taken.

Shutter Speed. Time the shutter is opened so that light can reach the film. Usually measured in fractions of one second.

Subject. The Object selected for emphasis in photo.

35 MM Camera. Any camera that exposes 35mm film.

View. That portion of the universe that is visible to the photographer at any given time.

Order Form:

Telephone orders: 1 (704) 369-8647

On- Line orders: pathway@dnet.net

Postal orders:
Soliloquy Press
383 Stamey Mountain Road
Franklin, NC 28734, USA.

Please send the following books:

Sales Tax:
Please add 6% for books shipped to NC address.

Shipping:
BookRate: $2.00 for first book, 75 cents for each additional book. (May take 3 to 4 weeks)
Air Mail: $3.50 per book.

Order Form:

Telephone orders: 1 (704) 369-8647

On- Line orders: pathway@dnet.net

Postal orders:
Soliloquy Press
383 Stamey Mountain Road
Franklin, NC 28734, USA.

Please send the following books:

Sales Tax:
Please add 6% for books shipped to NC address.

Shipping:
BookRate: $2.00 for first book, 75 cents for each additional book. (May take 3 to 4 weeks)
Air Mail: $3.50 per book.

Order Form:

Telephone orders: 1 (704) 369-8647

On- Line orders: pathway@dnet.net

Postal orders:
Soliloquy Press
383 Stamey Mountain Road
Franklin, NC 28734, USA.

Please send the following books:

Sales Tax:
Please add 6% for books shipped to NC address.

Shipping:
BookRate: $2.00 for first book, 75 cents for each additional book. (May take 3 to 4 weeks)
Air Mail: $3.50 per book.

Order Form:

Telephone orders: 1 (704) 369-8647

On- Line orders: pathway@dnet.net

Postal orders:
Soliloquy Press
383 Stamey Mountain Road
Franklin, NC 28734, USA.

Please send the following books:

Sales Tax:
Please add 6% for books shipped to NC address.

Shipping:
BookRate: $2.00 for first book, 75 cents for each additional book. (May take 3 to 4 weeks)
Air Mail: $3.50 per book.